PAR FOR LIFE

The Front Nine

by Kevin S. Paluch

with Jennifer Myers and Melanie Paluch

Published by Golf For Life, LLC. Par For Life series books my be purchased for educational, business or sales promotional use. Please contact the Par For Life Institute for more information:
1221 Geneva National Avenue South
Lake Geneva, Wisconsin, 53147
(262) 245-3020
www.ParForLife.com

The Par For Life program consists of exercise, nutritional and sports training information and recommendations. As with any exercise or nutritional program, you should consult your physician with any concerns prior to beginning. That said, you should also take personal responsibility of your own health in order to increase your longevity and your health-span. The information in this book should not be used to treat or to prevent medical conditions unless it is used with the full knowledge, compliance and agreement of personal physician or other licensed health care professional. Readers are strongly advised to seek the advice of their health care professional before proceeding with any changes in any health care program. This book is intended as an informational guide. The remedies, approaches, and techniques described herein are meant to supplement, and not to be a substitute for professional medical care or treatment. They should no be used to treat a serious ailment without prior consultation with a qualified health care professional.

First Printing, 2007
ISBN-13: 978-0-9794174-0-5
ISBN-10: 0-9794174-0-6
$19.95 US Dollars

From the Author...

Writing a book is a funny thing. You think it must be easy with all of your great ideas and knowledge. You read about the difficulties that others experience through the process and think you can do it better. Well, evidently some of those challenges are common to all authors, and I'm no exception. Even so, I wouldn't trade this for any other experience in life. My motivation to begin this journey began when a neurologist said, "Kevin, I'll give you 2 years before we have to fuse four of your neck vertebra together." Now, I've had a few wake up calls in life, but this one certainly rang in at volume level 10. It's been eight years since that day, and the new MRI's suggest a major change for the better, and I keep the old ones around to remind me of where I have been.

The journey to "self heal" sounded like a dream, but dreams do come true. Eight years later my neck is not perfect, however the bulging disks are minimal, symmetry is restored, and my neck is completely functional. I thought I was heading for a double bogey and it wound up a birdie. Just like in golf, in life you play one shot at a time and add them up at the end of the round.

My story has a fairytale outcome, and I believe yours can as well. Why Par for Life? In its simplest form, it is a program designed to allow you to play as much golf as you want for as long as you like. I watched my parents work their entire lives giving my brother and me opportunities to succeed, always thinking that someday they would finally get the chance to take up golf. The day eventually arrived - now they have the time to play the game, but the common aches and pains of "old age" have sneaked up on them, and their play has become limited. This does not need to be the case. Everyone should have the opportunity to play for years and years so that they become a member of the "Longevity Golf Club."

During my "self healing" days, I read and studied information regarding gaining flexibility, improving structural alignment, increasing strength, eating for proper nutrition, the importance of supplementation, the effects of body chemistry, and the tools to increasing longevity. Through these studies, accreditations, and certifications, the Par for Life program was developed.

There are many professionals I need to thank who have influenced the development of the Par for Life program. The three who have made the greatest impact are Dr. Michael Colgan, Peter Egoscue, and Cory Holly. The internationally acclaimed Dr. Colgan and the Colgan Institute has helped me both personally and professionally. Michael's best selling books, publications and Power Program development has and is changing the way nutrition, strength training, and the advancement of longevity is being viewed worldwide. I urge everyone to read and study his information at www.ColganInstitute.com. Peter Egoscue took one look at my posture and explained why I was having the neck and back problems that led me to the neurologist in the first place. I had the classic "In The Rough" posture, but not anymore. Pete's Egoscue Method has over one million pain free customers, and I am proud to be counted as one of them. If you're in pain, visit the Par for Life Institute or check out www.Egoscue.com and become pain free today. Cory Holly and the Cory Holly Institute gave me the education of a lifetime. The Institute is the premiere online international sports nutrition education center. His Certified Sports Nutrition Advisor program and monthly audio SNU program are a must for those interested in sports nutrition and athletic improvement. If you don't consider yourself an athlete, please do not count yourself out of experiencing his knowledge. Nutrition for athletes should read as optimum nutrition, and even the starchiest couch potato will benefit. If you don't go through the class, sign up for the SNU monthly audio program. The information is terrific and keeps you motivated. You will eagerly await your Sports Nutrition Update, and I encourage you to visit www.CoryHolly.com to sign up for his membership.

In addition to those three experts and friends, working with other professionals in various health fields have greatly affected my life. In my opinion, it is mandatory to seek out some good bodywork practitioners, and I have been lucky enough to work with some of the best you can find. If you ever find yourself located near these individuals, make the time for a session or two. If you're in the San Diego area call Stephen J. Bulger, HHP, or visit www.HellerWork.com. In Milwaukee, schedule a series with Brian Moore, www.Rolfing.com. Also in Milwaukee, see the extremely talented Andy Kerk, PT, OCS, ATC, CFMT, www.bMechanics.com. While Andy has many other credentials, he is the most talented osteopath in the business. We also believe in the benefits of a good chiropractor, but if yours is not also a Clinical Kinesiologist, consider finding one who is. We're lucky in the Lake Geneva, Wisconsin area to have Dr. LeRoy Moyer.

My twenty-five plus years as a PGA Golf Professional has been influenced greatly by three talented professionals. My first employment after college was working for Past PGA President, Tom Addis III. You will never meet a more organized professional in golf or any other industry. He instilled his wonderful gift with everyone lucky enough to work for him. After Tom, I had the great pleasure of working for the finest service oriented gentleman in the golf industry, Richard "Tag" Merritt. For 10 years I watched and learned how to teach and treat people under this accredited Professional. His desire to help students is unparalleled in the industry. If you're ever in San Diego, call Fairbanks Ranch Country Club and schedule an instant improvement in your game. Lastly, Tag's good friend Carl Welty made a tremendous impact on my knowledge of the golf swing. Carl has the largest video collection of the PGA Tour in the Country - second to none, and PGA Tour Professionals visit him on a regular basis.

It is rare in this day and age that employees work for the same company for over twenty years, yet I have been fortunate enough to work for Garth and Pamela Chambers for that period of time. They have allowed me to grow professionally as well as an individual. For those reasons alone I thank my lucky stars. I have been blessed with the environment and the relationship to be able to say that I love what I do and who I work for, and I am grateful to the Chambers for that.

To my parents, Edward and Joan Paluch, I might not have made the PGA Tour, however, the contribution I have made and inspired in the community has made a difference in many lives. I believe this will probably be my greatest success, and I couldn't have done any of it without a great upbringing from wonderful parents.

To my good friend and co-author, Jennifer, I cannot thank you enough for your talent, abilities, and listening skills. Jennifer kept us on track throughout the process, and made writing an easy business. She's an exceptional person. I look forward to our next several books.

I thank Geneva National Golf Club in Lake Geneva, Wisconsin, for allowing us to use their facilities and photography for this project. If you're ever in the Milwaukee or Chicago area, the short trip to visit these three courses designed by Arnold Palmer, Lee Trevino and Gary Player is a must on your itinerary.

And lastly I need to thank my wife Melanie (the Chef of our book) and daughter Jordan for putting up with a Crusader. When you're on a crusade, you're not always fun to be around. I am blessed with a great family, and writing this book with them was an enjoyable experience.

Please enjoy, and go for Par For Life,
Kevin S. Paluch

Par For Life... The Front Nine

We golfers are quite a breed. You could work with a person for five years and never know that they play racquet ball or bowl once a week, but EVERYONE knows that we are golfers. For gifts we get golf stuff – clothes, books, toys, equipment, you name it – and we love it. If we're channel surfing, we pause (if not stop for hours) on any golf event. The game comes up in conversation at every social event we attend. We live and breathe the game – we're golfers! You're a golf nut, admit it and embrace it.

So, why combine our love of golf, health, cooking and nutrition all in one book? Because we are as interested in creating lifelong health and vitality as we are in hitting a little white ball into a hole eighteen times. The Par For Life Institute offers programs designed to accelerate your progress and extend the longevity of your golf game, and the combination of functional golf instruction and nutrition principles is the prefect way to illustrate our programs in one book. The food that you put in your body can make an incredibly positive impact on your health. The activities that you engage your body in can make an incredibly positive impact on your well being. Put these two basic principles together, and we aim to help you transform your body into a vessel that will allow you to golf as much as you want for as long as you like. Our goal at the Par For Life Institute is to bring you Function, Strength, Nutrition and Longevity, and following to the information in this book will serve to deliver all of these.

This book will share with you some of our favorite recipes to take you from morning to night, on the tee or not. We also share simple exercises that we find vital in preparing our bodies to perform the golf swing, and lessons on how to perform a functional golf swing. Add to these our Front Nine Principles to a healthy longevity, and there you have it – all of our passions rolled together in our first Par For Life Book.

Enjoy! See you on the first tee.

The Par For Life Institute exists to provide instruction, education, products and services that will allow you to play as much golf as you want for as long as you like.

The game of golf is one of the few sports that can be played from "cradle to grave." Golf naturally adjusts through handicaps and course settings to provide both challenge and enjoyment as a golfer learns the game, improves and ages. The programs offered through the Par For Life Institute will rejuvinate the golf industry by empowering golfers with tools and knowledge to defy the effects of aging and play golf for a lifetime.

www.ParForLife.com

PAR FOR LIFE

The Front Nine

Player #1
Geneva National Golf Club, Lake Geneva, Wisconsin

The Front Nine –
Par For Life's Principles For Life

Our Front Nine principles are the basic building blocks for a healthy lifestyle. The prevailing actuary tables would have you believe that we should live to be about eighty, with aches and pains beginning in our forties and chronic health concerns a constant after fifty. This is a farce. There's no reason why we shouldn't live to be 100 and able to do everything we want, including playing golf & shooting our age! Following the advice of our Front Nine Principles will help us all achieve a long, happy and healthy life.

The goal of the Par For Life Institute is to bring you Function, Strength, Nutrition and Longevity. By design, our Front Nine focuses mostly on Function and Nutrition, as these lead to Strength and Longevity. We define function simply as the ability to move through and enjoy the activities in your life that you need to do as well as those you wish to do, without pain or discomfort. Functional Golf is creating a golf swing that enables the body to be in a stable and strong position to effectively be able to smoothly transfer weight back and through the swing, without generating aches and pains during or after a round.

In Nutrition, we strive for optimal levels of vitamins, minerals and other elements that lead to a healthy Longevity. Most government regulated nutrition labels on foods and supplements give us the appearance that we are getting 100% of our necessary nutrients, but these levels are the minimums that are needed to prevent diseases borne from malnutrition, not the optimal levels that our bodies crave, and certainly not the levels needed to maintain an active or athletic lifestyle. The foods and supplement levels we advocate throughout this book and through the Par For Life Institute are recommended for anyone looking to live a long and healthy life.

Without Function, the Strength we gain can lead to structural problems, and without the combination of Function, Strength and Nutrition, a healthy Longevity is unattainable. We want you to achieve all four of our goals, so that you can, among other things, play as much golf as you want for as long as you like.

The Front Nine is more than just a cookbook, more than just a nutritional guide, more than just an exercise program, and more than just golf instruction. The sum of the parts create something greater. To use this book, look to the recipes as you would in any other cookbook. Look to the outsides of each page however, to follow us through a process of making your body healthy, creating a more functional and stronger structure to begin from, and play golf in a more consistent manner for the rest of your life.

The Front Nine - #1

Start Each and Every Day with Your Par for Life Exercise Recipe

The body's design calls for some very basic alignment principles, and our first aim is to make sure that our golfers show these alignments. To simplify the human form, when one is viewed from the side, we should be able to draw a perfect plumb line through their ear, shoulder, hip, knee and ankle. Furthermore, the line should fall through the joints on the right side of the body in the same manner that it falls on the left. Viewed from the front, in addition to this plumb line, we should be able to draw perfect horizontal lines from ear to ear, shoulder to shoulder, hip to hip and knee to knee.

Though this is our intended design our joints fall out of proper alignment due to a combination of habit, sport, activity, work, inactivity, child bearing, poor nutrition and injury. These misalignments lead to compensating movements which then lead to more misalignments. The result is a steady decline in sport performance and inevitable aches and pains that we incorrectly attribute to a natural effect of aging,

Starting every day with your Par For Life Recipe of exercises will serve to reposition your joints into vertical and horizontal alignment. Once in alignment you will not only gain function, but greatly if not entirely reduce the aches and pains you are now experiencing, or prevent the ones you are now unknowingly on your way to developing. Through the process of these exercises, you will gain strength which will further improve your form and function and prove to safeguard yourself against future injuries and discomfort. These exercises may save your life, prevent disease, and allow you to minimize annoying joint problems in your life.

Throughout this book we offer some general exercise recipes for you to perform as you start your day, warm up before you tee off, stay limber throughout your round and end your day in a better postural position.

As good as these exercise recipes are, however, this general series will not be able to give you the extreme benefit you will gain if you receive a personalized postural assessment and exercise program designed to address and improve your specific postural deviations and dysfunctions.

For more information on a personal assessment, please visit the Par For Life Institute's website at www.ParForLife.com.

The Front Nine - #2

EAT ORGANIC, UNPROCESSED FOODS & TAKE YOUR ESSENTIAL FATTY ACIDS DAILY

Organic foods are grown and raised on land and feed that is free of chemicals, pesticides and hormones. The soil on an organic farm is full of nutrients and trace minerals through crop rotation rather than chemical manipulation. The end result is food rich in the vitamins and minerals that nature intended.

We have heard organic nay-sayers comment that mass produced foods are good enough, and that the government would not allow harmful chemicals into our foods. If this is your position, we challenge you to visit the EPA's website, type in carcinogens, and see all of the pesticides, herbicides and fungicides that pop up. The numbers are staggering, even if you only look at the chemicals that are legally used in farms today. Organic food is produced without the use of any of these chemicals, and even if some chemicals are deemed "safe" in small quantities, why risk the exposure?

Chemicals and nutrients aside, organic foods simply taste better. When you are looking though the produce section, you may notice that the non-organic oranges are just a bit brighter, the cucumbers shinier and the bananas bigger. All of these apparent benefits are nothing but cosmetics for fruits and vegetables. Since we grow our food with insufficient nutrients, we make up for the deficiencies with wax, edible pigment and genetic manipulation. An organic orange tastes like a fresh orange – every time. An organic tomato tastes like you remember tomatoes tasting fresh from the garden. Organic foods taste the way nature intended, and Mother Nature did not get it wrong.

On to fats. Alpha-Linolenic (Omega 3) and Linoleic (Omega 6) essential fatty acids are not able to be produced in our bodies and must be supplied from our diet. The role of these fats is so enormous that you should never go a day without them. Make sure your daily mineral and vitamin pack includes EPA and DHA. In addition to these, supplement your diet with flax seed oil and, for those over forty, borage oil. Eat the right fish - wild is always best - on a regular basis. Three ounces of wild salmon or 4 ounces of sardines contain up to 1 full gram of Omega 3 fatty acids. In many studies, it has been shown that Eskimos have a very low incidence of coronary disease event though they tend to be overweight and have a high fat diet. The difference may be that they consume the right fats, and we should too.

The Front Nine - #3
TAKE A COMPLETE MINERAL, VITAMIN AND ANTIOXIDANT FORMULA EVERY DAY

We have been given a great disservice when we have been told by doctors and dieticians that eating a "balanced" diet is all we need, and additional supplements are not worth the time or the expense. The truth is that our food sources in America today are so devoid of their original nutrients and our environment so polluted that it is nearly impossible to achieve optimal nutrition without assistance. Even if you were lucky enough to eat nothing but fresh organic foods, you would have little chance of providing your body with all of the nutrients it truly craves.

In addition to our basic vitamin and mineral needs, other factors such as our environment, lifestyle and our frequency, duration and intensity of exercise will cause oxidation in our cells. Powerful antioxidants are essential to keep our bodies from rusting out.

Before perusing the grocery store aisle, please do some research about the bioavailability and quality of the supplement you choose, and know that you get what you pay for. Many mass produced commercial brands are used by doctors to follow your GI tract - they are so useless that they can travel through your body and exit with the lettering still intact. We advocate also taking the time to research the scientist responsible for the creation of the formula, and the rationale behind the combinations. If you don't know where to start, we may be one resource for you by visiting our website at www.ParForLife.com. You could also look for advice at a reputable health food store or wellness center. Take care, however, to avoid a dietician who only sells one brand of vitamins, and the formula is not fully disclosed. Also do your best to avoid the magic bullet hype. There is no such thing as one element that will cure all of your ills and create instant health, and if someone tries to sell you something that does, strongly consider spending your money elsewhere.

So, our position is that it is absolutely essential that we feed our bodies with the nutrients we need by not only eating fresh, natural foods, but by taking a complete mineral, vitamin and antioxidant formula every day. Find the right, high quality formula for you, considering your lifestyle and your sport, and your body will thank you for years to come.

The Front Nine - #4

Eat Quality Protein with Every Meal and as a Snack

Eating quality protein throughout the day provides your body with pure building blocks to grow muscle and restore your energy levels. Though its so essential, many people find that the amount of protein they consume compared to the optimal amount they should receive is often far different.

Start each day with a protein shake made with fresh squeezed fruit juice, flax seed oil, filtered or distilled water and whey protein isolate. A complete whey protein isolate is the best protein available, and make sure yours has all of the essential amino acids. Using fresh squeezed juice as opposed to packaged juice from a carton will serve to stabilize your blood sugar and insulin levels, promote an alkaline environment and provide plenty of beneficial enzymes and antioxidants. Fresh squeezed juice differs from packaged juice in more ways than just taste. When you juice fruits and vegetables, the sugars are actually very low on the glycemic index, and the enzymes that are so vital to their beneficial effects quickly dissipate. By the time juice is pasteurized and package, these enzymes are all but gone, and, when it comes to insulin reactions, the sugar in the packaged juice is only a little better than refined white sugar. Finally, the flax seed oil provides Omega 3 fatty acids, which help to improve joint and circulation function.

We choose whey-protein isolate over other powdered proteins because it is known as the highest quality protein available for its growth promotion, nitrogen retention and biological value. Whey protein isolate is a complete protein, yielding a full spectrum of both essential and non-essential amino acids. It is digested faster, has more positive effects on your immune system, and may have more anti-carcinogenic effects than other forms of protein. Look to our breakfast section for more information on whey-protein isolate.

After breakfast, continue to feed your body good protein throughout the day. We are not advocating a no or low carbohydrate diet - we need carbohydrates as well as fats and proteins. We do, however, encourage a higher protein balance in your diet, particularly for the majority of us who do not have the natural metabolism that allows one to eat whatever they like and remain thin. It's always been easy to plan protein in meals, but snacking tends to be a carb feast. Snacks can be an easy way to add protein, if you take some time to plan.

Look for protein filled snacks in a dozen raw unsalted almonds, a slice of organic roasted turkey or a small scoop of chicken salad. At any rate, drop the trans fat full chips and choose a higher quality snack.

The Front Nine - #5

DON'T SPIKE YOUR INSULIN, AVOID SUGARY FOODS AND
CHOOSE LOW GLYCEMIC FOODS

Diabetes has to be the epidemic of the century. It's very possible it will take down our health care system and this doesn't need to be the case. This is just another example of another man made disease. Furthermore, the term "adult onset" is becoming a misnomer. One in four children with diabetes actually has Type 2, diet and weight related, diabetes. This phenomenon was virtually unheard of even ten years ago.

In addition to keeping obesity in check, Par For Life is a big proponent of avoiding foods that will spike your insulin, even for those of us with normal body weights. Until very recently, science believed that taking protein with each meal slows down the assimilation of carbohydrates in your system, thus stabilizing your blood sugar and insulin level. We now believe that this is not the case, and avoiding processed sugars must be a primary goal.

When we talk about high versus low glycemic foods, we are discussing how your body, particularly your insulin production, reacts to sugars coming into your bloodstream. Technically, you could have two foods with the exact same calories and grams of sugars and carbohydrates, but one with a low glycemic index and one with a high index. Your body will have little insulin reaction to the item low on the scale, and the high index food will cause an insulin spike. Your goal should be to maintain a fairly even pattern of sugars and insulin in your bloodstream, avoiding spikes and dips throughout the day. We suggest eating some fruit early in the day, and sticking to low-glycemic foods after 4pm to ensure a good night's sleep.

Many non-golfers think of golfing as a walk in the park. Those of use who take the game seriously, however, understand the physical demands of the sport. Though we don't often work up a sweat on the course (and electrolyte replacing sports beverages are seldom necessary), keeping your insulin levels steady throughout your round will improve your game. On the course, reach for a bottle of water and a protein snack, and skip the soda and candy bar.

In short, don't spike your insulin - slow and steady wins the race.

The Front Nine - #6

KEEP WELL HYDRATED

It seems to be common knowledge that drinking 6 to 8 glasses of water each day is enough to stay properly hydrated. What is not so commonly known is that even this healthy amount may be inadequate for many people.

At the Par for Life Institute we measure each client's intra and extra cellular water levels using our calibrated Bio-Impedance Analyzer. To date, our clients and other populations using the machine show that less than 10% of us are properly hydrated. Clean water is essential for every cell in your body - important to breathe, digest, eliminate, perspire, keep tall, produce blood and maintain tissue, not to mention being able to function as a body in motion. Drinking enough water is also one of those simple cause and effect things – when you drink more you feel better, and you tend to feel worse when you are dehydrated.

Drinking more water alone may not get your body to optimum hydration. If you carry a low percentage of muscle mass and a high percentage of body fat, it is very difficult to maintain a healthy hydration level. Extra-cellular water is what is quickly eliminated, and your intra-cellular water is what will maintain proper hydration over time. It is estimated that a fat cell can only hold up to 15% water, while a muscle cell can hold closer to 70% water. Knowing that, it is an easy jump to say that the leaner you stay, the better chance you have of holding more intra-cellular water and being properly hydrated throughout your day.

Try not to fight your own progress, either. Excessive caffeine, sugars and other additives to drinks can tend to be de-hydrating. The Par For Life Institute would never suggest dropping coffee out of your repertoire, we like a cup or two ourselves. That being said, there's no substitute for good, clean water, and, before your morning coffee, you will do your body well to first drink a large glass of water. Find a great water bottle that you can keep with you and refill often throughout the day.

When you choose your water, distilled is the best way to go, and reverse osmosis is the next best choice. Every month you can find an article in any number of publications relating reports of the dangers of contaminated water. We have found that the absolute safest and purest water is distilled. In our homes we make it daily. At work, we buy distilled water for our coolers. For those of you who are looking to your water for minerals, stop - look to your diet and supplements for that - choose distilled.

The Front Nine - #7
SAVE YOUR MIRACLE BRAIN

New ways to enhance memory and increase brain capacity seem to make headlines every week. There has been tremendous scientific progress made to date and numerous books and articles on the subject. We suggest you keep your mind active and read a few of them.

In so many ways, the brain is exactly like the rest of the body. It needs to receive an ample supply of vitamins and minerals in order to survive and thrive. Eat to save your brain and make sure you are getting the right antioxidants to combat free radical damage in our most precious organ.

The latest science is telling us that brain cells do not normally divide and replicate like cells in other areas of the body. This means that when damage occurs, it tends to be permanent. When we talk about damage, we are not limiting the scope to head injuries. Simple brain oxidation, the enemy that our antioxidants combat, is responsible for nearly all of the non-injury damage to the brain. Genetics play a minute part in this brain degeneration when compared to oxidation. This problem begins after the age of 25, and progresses at different rates depending on an individual's environment and nutritional habits. No matter what your age, however, its never too late to begin to reduce the free radical damage in your brain, and there may be nothing more important to your longevity.

In addition to antioxidants, hormones and fats play a vital role in brain health, and heredity appears to play a surprisingly small role. While we will not delve into the subject of brain related hormones in the Front Nine, we would encourage you to look into the effects of Dopamine and Serotonin and how their levels naturally reduce with age. A diet rich in the "right" fats is also essential to maintaining this fatty organ; our brains are comprised of roughly 60% fat. Ensuring that you are taking in a healthy amount of essential fatty acids and antioxidants, while limiting your consumption of trans fats and saturated fats will serve your brain, and your waistline, well.

Though we study and talk about nutrition as it relates to brain health a lot, we would be doing you a great disservice if we did not defer to an expert. For more information on saving your "miracle brain", purchase a copy of Dr. Michael Colgan's "Save Your Brain" today.

The Front Nine - #8
REACH A HIGHER LEVEL OF HEALTH WITH STRENGTH TRAINING

The benefits of participating in regular weight bearing exercise are immense: healthy joints, increased lean body mass, a stronger immune system, increased bone density, improved brain function, accelerated fat burning, improved posture, better sleep, disease reduction, increased metabolic rate, hormone stabilization, greater energy levels and more. We could go on and on, but you probably get the point. With all of these benefits it's clear that any good longevity strategy must include weight bearing exercise.

Not all weight lifting, however, is created equally. At the Par For Life Institute, we advocate Functional Progressive Resistance Training (FPRT), which is weight bearing exercise designed with free movement in mind. Rather than sitting in a machine, we want you to move as you would in your sport and other life activities in order to build all of your stabilizing muscles, link the muscle chains throughout your body, and stabilize your joints.

Our favorite equipment for functional weight training is a cross-cable machine or, better yet, a quad-cable machine (similar to a regular cross cable, but with four weight stacks). Cable machines do a terrific job of creating a free motion workout which is designed to match the body's natural design of motion. Work with a personal trainer to design a program to match your needs and sport. For examples of great cable machine work-outs, look to the Par For Life Institute's website at www.ParForLife.com, or consider purchasing a copy of Dr. Michael Colgan's Power Program. If you do not have access to a gym and cables are not available, free weights (dumbells) are the next best thing.

For an injury free workout we recommend beginning with a brief Par For Life Recipe to get your body into a better alignment, followed by a cardio workout until you break a sweat, and then begin your progressive weight training. Finish with a stretch or a second exercise recipe. Working out in this fashion will keep you injury free and feeling great.

For the serious athlete, periodize your workouts. We'll discuss more of this in The Back Nine when we focus on improving your strength, skill, balance, structure, health, and more. However, the evidence is clear that overtraining is like most things in life - too much of a good thing could become detrimental.

Strengthen your body, keep it functional, moving and strong, and every aspect of your life will benefit from it.

The Front Nine - #9

SETTING YOURSELF UP FOR A LIFETIME - THE PROPER ADDRESS POSITION

Have you ever listened to Tiger Woods discuss the golf swing? Year after year this icon talks about his continual effort to perfect his address position. The set-up or address position could be the most critical component of the golf swing, and to get it right, you need to work toward perfecting your posture and alignment.

The proper address position sets you up for consistency and success and allows your body to correctly perform the dynamic weight transfer necessary to produce a good golf swing. It is this weight transfer that creates a consistent pattern of motion through the hit and release of the swing. Being able to repeat this pattern of motion throughout the course of a round of golf is the goal of all great players. Jack Nicklaus once said, "Golf is a game of misses. Whoever misses it best usually wins." Avoid swing compensations by getting your set-up correct, and you just may start missing better.

Looking from the front view, the golfer's address posture should display vertical lines through their shoulders, hips, knees and ankles, and the right and left sides of the body should have horizontal lines through those joints at ninety-degrees to the vertical. Having your feet up to shoulder width apart is acceptable, but going wider than that defies your natural form. We'll discuss these lines throughout the book.

From the side view, the golfers address posture should show a slight bend in the knee, toes pointed straight forward or everted no more than five degrees, and a tilt from the hips with a relaxed shoulder position that maintains the proper s-curve of your spine.

Many instructors will tell students to drop a shoulder and place your feet in a wide stance with your toes pointed outward. From the side view they may say to reach down on the club, which results in your shoulders and low back rounding. They do this not out of ignorance, but simply out of an unspoken understanding that the average golfer is unable to achieve and consistently maintain the proper address position. Consequently, rather than frustrating the student with instructions that they cannot perform, they teach compensations that let them hit the ball with some success.

We call this Compensational Golf, and find that it is far more prevalent than Functional Golf. This was our calling to develop and promote the methods of the Par For Life Institute. Our goal is to deliver to our students tools and knowledge that allows them to improve the condition of their bodies, which then allows them to achieve a more functional address position and swing, leading to better, painless, Functional golf, giving them the ability to golf as much as they want for as long as they like.

The Front Nine

HOW TO USE THIS BOOK

In using this book, we encourage you to do more than just look for a recipe or a golf tip that suits you. The pages in The Front Nine are a combination of three synergistic stories.

Toward the center of every page you will find recipes that we have found to be tasty and healthy, and all of them refer back in some way to one of our Front Nine Principles. You will find extra boxes, offering helpful tips on nutrition, cooking and life. By the way, the pictures of our recipes are all real food... many food photographers use tricks like glue & soap bubbles to make their food look tastier. We believe food can look good, taste good, and promote your health and longevity all at the same time.

The outer side of the right hand pages are dedicated to our Par For Life golf instruction, progressing you through grip, set-up, full swing, short game and putting.

On the outer side of the left hand pages you will find the progression of our postural and exercise recipes that are designed to get your body completely functional and better able to perform on the golf course and in life.

The three stories all live together and refer to each other. Enjoy the book, and go for Par For Life.

The Clubhouse
Geneva National Golf Club, Lake Geneva, Wisconsin

Breakfast & Grip

Your mother was right - Breakfast is the most important meal of the day!

The origin of the word breakfast is to "Break the Fast" you have been on since the night before. Your body is hungry to start the day - do it in a way that helps you nourish yourself right through lunch.

At the Par For Life Institute, we advocate starting your day with a full serving of protein and going easy on the carbohydrates. A great way to do this is with a shake or smoothie using fresh squeezed organic fruit juice, distilled water, flax seed oil and whey protein isolate. In addition to your shake, take care not to forget your daily vitamins, minerals and antioxidants.

If you are entertaining or looking for a more substantial meal than a shake or smoothie, be sure to try to get a good balance of protein to start the day off right to nourish your body and feed your structure.

Its not only your food that starts the day off right - make sure you take your body through a full range of motion, The intensity is up to you, but you need to move if you want to make Par For Life!

Player #2
Geneva National Golf Club
Lake Geneva, Wisconsin

Protein Shakes...

Start your day with a tasty and healthy shake that centers around whey protein isolate as its base.

All proteins are not created the same. Whey protein isolate was developed for its awesome properties to restore and heal the body. The isolate was developed specifically for cancer and other critical patients who were in desperate need for pure nourishment, but whose appetites were so ravaged by their disease that they would not eat well. Whey protein isolate is now widely available for the general healthy population, and the benefits it will offer you will not be disappointing.

Benefits of consuming a liquid protein shake rather than other forms of protein include that it is better assimilated into the bloodstream, easier to digest than solid proteins requiring less enzyme assistance, poses less allergen threats, serves as a great treat for kids and adults, and it tastes great!

Through this section you will find some great suggestions for shakes. If you would like to try your own concoctions, please do, and follow these simple steps:

...The Perfect Start of the Day

1 - Decide on a liquid to use as the base of your shake. You can use distilled water, non-fat milk, fresh squeezed orange juice (not from a carton), soy milk, or rice milk. You might check your blood type to see which liquid is most agreeable with your body, but we recommend the fresh juice or water.

2 – Add your favorite whey protein isolate powder. There are several good ones on the market to choose from, however do your homework to make sure you're getting the best formula possible. Make sure your choice includes a full spectrum of essential amino acids, is produced and designed without being subjected to high heat, and is lightly sweetened with Stevia or Splenda® rather than refined sugar, corn syrup or an artificial sweetener.

3 – Add the good fats to your shake. One tablespoon of flax seed oil, and, for those over forty, one tablespoon of borage seed oil will give you a dose of the essential fatty acids that our bodies cannot make on their own.

4 – Add a cup of fresh or frozen fruit as your carbohydrate. You will find that many of our shakes include a frozen banana. This gives us a great consistency and the chill we like without adding ice.

5 – Add additional ingredients to improve your health and immune system. Ingredients might include some the following: Vitamin C, Creatine Monohydrate, a green blend, raw honey, L-Glutamine, D-Ribose, or bee pollen. In adding these supplements, we encourage you to consult a professional to look at these in conjunction with your other vitamin and mineral supplements to ensure proper dosage.

Another important note - always use fresh squeezed juice. We find fresh orange juice tastes best with the most combinations, but fresh grapefruit or apple juice also lends themselves well to many flavors (though if you take daily medications, please avoid the grapefruit juice). When we say fresh – we mean fresh! Squeeze it yourself and use it within the hour. The difference to your body is much greater than just the better taste. A glass of packaged orange juice has little in the way of beneficial enzymes. It also tends to be acidic in nature and the high glycemic index will serve to spike your insulin. On the contrary, a glass of fresh squeezed orange juice, is full of beneficial enzymes, low on the glycemic scale and actually is an alkaline food.

The following pages offer suggestions and recipes for our favorite shakes. Feel free to experiment and make your own!

Happy Joint Juice

1 scoop vanilla whey protein isolate powder
4 oz fresh squeezed orange juice
1 tablespoon flax seed oil
1 tablespoon borage oil
½ cup pineapple
¼ lemon, squeezed (optional)
¼ cup frozen blueberries

Chocolate-Banana-Strawberry

1 scoop chocolate whey protein isolate powder
4 oz fresh squeezed orange juice
1 tablespoon flax seed oil
1 tablespoon borage oil
½ semi-ripe frozen banana
¼ cup strawberries

The core principle of Par For Life is to teach and promote "Functional Golf". To do that, we need to get you off of the golf course, pry the club out of your hand, and take some time addressing the basic design of the human body - how it functions and looks in an ideal situation.

First we address your posture. To many people, thinking of posture brings back memories of your grandmother admonishing you to sit up straight at the dinner table, or visions of models walking with books on their heads... Forget all that - we look at how your joints line up in relationship to each other and to ninety degree angles.

The banana is a versatile fruit. It is easily digested, rarely causes allergies and contains natural sugars (sucrose, fructose and glucose) which are released quickly into the bloodstream, giving you instant energy.

Bananas are most known for being a great source of potassium. Potassium is an essential electrolyte that helps to regulate your blood chemistry. Without potassium working together with sodium, your muscles stop firing correctly, and your metabolism is adversely affected. In addition to potassium, bananas are rich in vitamins B6 and C, they're self contained & tasty!

Chocolate-Banana-Almond

1 scoop chocolate whey protein isolate powder
4 oz fresh squeezed orange juice
1 tablespoon flax seed oil
1 tablespoon borage oil
½ semi ripe frozen banana
1 tablespoon almond butter
¼ cup strawberries

Cinnamon Almond

1 scoop vanilla whey protein isolate powder
4 oz fresh squeezed orange juice
1 tablespoon flax seed oil
1 tablespoon borage oil
¼ cup frozen peach or apricot
¼ cup raw almonds
$\frac{1}{8}$ teaspoon cinnamon

Brain Power

1 scoop chocolate or vanilla whey protein isolate powder
4 oz fresh squeezed orange juice
1 tablespoon flax seed oil
1 tablespoon borage oil
½ cup frozen blueberries
¼ lemon, squeezed
May add chopped pear or banana

Pineapple contains the protein digesting enzyme bromelain. It affects protein turnover in the body including proteins found in joint tissue, as well as enhancing absorption of nutrients such as glucosamine, sulfur, and bioflavanoids. For a quick and simple snack, cut fresh pineapple and sprinkle with fresh ground pepper. Really - try it.

There are a lot of books out there designed to teach you the game of golf. Nearly every golf book or instructional manual you pick up will make a huge assumption before even beginning – that every reader will be able to perform every move the book describes.

We know that this is not the case. We will offer what we call Functional Golf instruction, designed to teach real people, with real bodies how to improve their game. The right and left sides of this book, although different, are not unrelated to each other. To the contrary, in order to really affect your golf game and defy the aches, pains and performance declines of aging, paying attention to both sides of this book are critical.

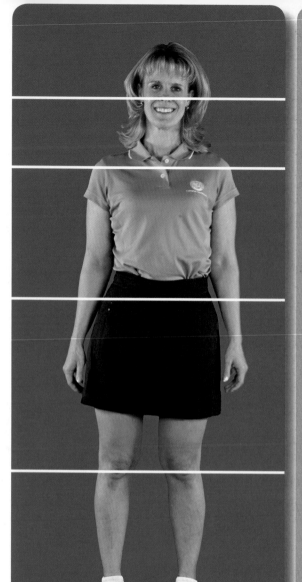

When we look at a person's posture, we look for simple lines and right angles. Though we simplify things a bit, on a picture of the front view of a person with "perfect" posture, we should be able to draw horizontal lines through the ears, the shoulders, the hips and the knees, and these lines should bisect the joint in the same spot on both sides of the body. A vertical line bisecting the body should show symmetry with the right and left sides.

In this example, you can see that the right hip and left shoulder are elevated in relationship to their partner.

The blueberries' skin is a very valuable nutrient. This pigment is a powerful antioxidant, fighting off disease and also cancer. Blueberries have the highest antioxidant capacity because of their large anthocyanin concentration. Blueberries are not only a powerful antioxidant but also have been proved to preserve vision, particularly as an extract supplement. Finding blueberries in cooler climates during the winter can be expensive. Try freezing berries while they're in season.

Shakes & Smoothies

Vanilla Mango Whip

1 scoop vanilla whey protein isolate powder
4 oz fresh squeezed orange juice
1 tablespoon flax seed oil
1 tablespoon borage oil
½ cup mango
¼ lime, squeezed
¼ cup organic apple juice

Strawberry-Chocolate Vitamin C

1 scoop chocolate whey protein isolate powder
4 oz fresh squeezed orange juice
1 tablespoon flax seed oil
1 tablespoon borage oil
½ cup strawberries
¼ lemon, squeezed
1 tablespoon raw organic honey

Papaya Digestive Drink

1 scoop chocolate or vanilla whey protein isolate powder
4 oz fresh squeezed orange juice
1 tablespoon flax seed oil
1 tablespoon borage oil
½ cup papaya
¼ lime, squeezed

Kiwi Immune Boost

1 scoop vanilla whey protein isolate powder
4 oz fresh squeezed orange or grapefruit juice
1 tablespoon flax seed oil
1 tablespoon borage oil
2 kiwi's, peeled
½ lemon, squeezed

An Apple a Day...

1 scoop vanilla whey protein isolate powder
4 oz fresh squeezed orange juice
1 tablespoon flax seed oil
1 tablespoon borage oil
½ cup apple
1 tablespoon organic honey
¼ lemon, squeezed

Strawberries are an excellent source of vitamin C. A serving of eight strawberries contains about 50 calories and offers a good source of natural fiber.
Kiwi is also high in vitamin C and fiber, as well as potassium. Go on the internet & do a search on the kiwi fruit, and you can find numerous studies and claims of the kiwi's role in cancer and heart disease prevention. What we do know for sure - they're tasty!

Like many books on golf instruction, we begin with a discussion on your Grip. Don't close the book too soon... our similarities will end there.

Grip is, of course, an important element of a functional golf swing – the critical link between the golfer and the club. Through this first chapter, we will discuss how to grip your club and the three most commonly used styles. Whichever grip you choose, based on your comfort and results, make sure your hands have a firm yet supple hold on the club. White knuckles are for roller coasters and driving with teenagers - not for the golf course.

The common idea that a good grip will create a good swing unfortunately discounts the fact that your swing can only be as good as your physical abilities allow. Golfers generally choose their grip style based on what is most comfortable and in the manner which best allows them to square up the club face to the target at impact.

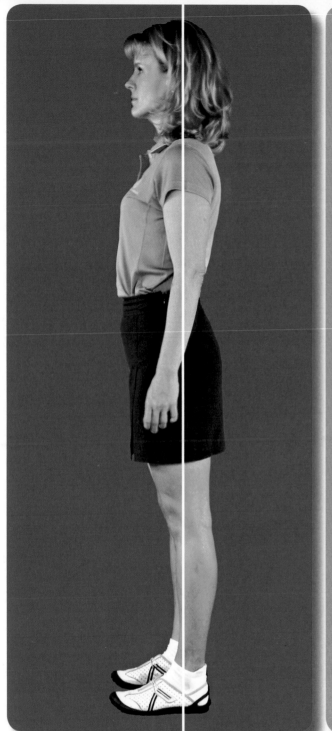

From the side view, we should be able to draw a plumb line straight up from just forward of the ankle bone, through the knee, hip, shoulder and ear.

Comparing this line on the right and left sides of the body should show identical joint positions.

Before we move on to how nearly every person falls short of this ideal to some degree, please note that we simplify the body's design with our lines, but for our purposes, these simplifications serve us well.

Flax seed and borage oils are rich in Omega 3, Omega 6 and GLA fats, and serve your body well in reducing chronic inflamation. Flax or borage oils can not be cooked at high temperatures. Use them for dressings, shakes, and after cooking additions like pasta.

Shakes & Smoothies

Melon Ball

1 scoop vanilla whey protein isolate powder
4 oz fresh squeezed orange juice
1 tablespoon flax seed oil
1 tablespoon borage oil
¼ cup watermelon
¼ cup cantelope or other melon

Apricot Almond Smoothie

1 scoop vanilla whey protein isolate powder
4 oz fresh squeezed orange juice
1 tablespoon flax seed oil
1 tablespoon borage oil
½ cup apricots
1 tablespoon organic almond butter
6-8 raw almonds

Sleepy Banana

1 scoop vanilla or chocolate whey protein isolate powder
4 oz fresh squeezed orange juice
1 tablespoon flax seed oil
1 tablespoon borage oil
1 semi ripe banana
¼ lemon, squeezed
¼ cup live culture, organic low-fat yogurt

Stimulating Chocolate Coffee

1 scoop vanilla or chocolate whey protein isolate powder
4 oz fresh squeezed orange juice
1 tablespoon flax seed oil
1 tablespoon borage oil
1-2 teaspoons instant coffee or
    ¼ cup cold espresso
½ semi ripe frozen banana

We expect that our Par For Life clients will also choose the most comfortable grip, but caution that as your body's function changes and improves, you may find that your grip may change as well.

The goal of a good grip is to unify the movement of the hands, allowing for additional leverage and power to be used in the swing. This leverage, created by the wrist cocking or hinging, increases the velocity of club head. Knowing that the speed of your club head is the most important variable for creating distance, grip is important to getting the ball down the fairway.

The grip you choose allows you to use the power generated by the motion of your body through the release of your hands and arms. Since becoming more functional through targeted stretches and exercises will improve your function, your grip may change, and your ability to release your hands will also improve. As your release gets better, so will your consistency and accuracy on the course - maybe even adding a few yards to your shots.

When choosing a nut for a recipe or a snack, always look for raw, unsalted nuts. They provide antioxidants and have anti-inflammatory properties. Not only are raw nuts high in protein and essential fatty acids, various studies have indicated that, when eaten in moderation, raw nuts may help decrease the risk of cancer, heart disease and diabetes.
Raw is the key. As in any food, exposure to heat, light and air oxidizes fat cells, negating all of their inherent benefits.

Confused by all of the talk about caffeine or no caffeine? The Par For Life Institute takes the same stance on caffeine as we do with sugar & alcohol - take it in moderation. If its something you like to have, have it. Coffee in itself can be acidic. Even so, who can resist a great cup of coffee? Stick to the Par For Life principles and buy organic coffees. You will find that they are more alkaline than their commercially produced cousins, and any time you can cut the acidity in your foods is good.

Unfortunately, nearly all of us fall short of the perfect posture goal. We look at four joints (ankles, knees, hips and shoulders) as well as the head position. Each joint can be high or low, forward or back, or inside or outside of the proper line, and the two sides of the body's joints can show different deviations. That being said, there are hundreds and hundreds of different combinations of posture problems. Rather than overwhelming everyone with all of the possibilities, we group people into three basic categories in an effort to improve their position.

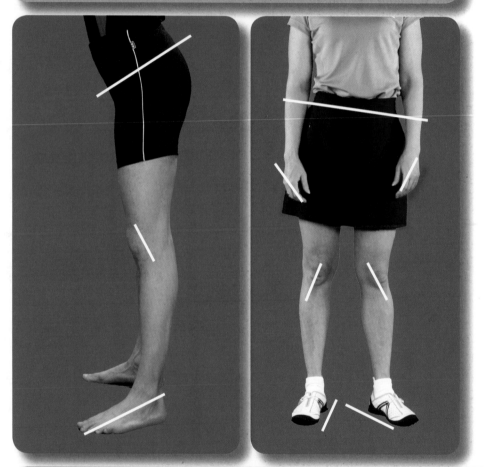

1 ¼ cup whole wheat pastry flour
⅓ cup uncooked farina
1 scoop vanilla whey protein
   isolate powder
⅓ cup Splenda®
1 teaspoon baking soda
1 teaspoon baking powder
½ teaspoon salt (optional)

1 ½ cups vanilla soy milk
¼ cup applesauce
¼ cup egg substitute
Cooking spray
½ cup coarsely chopped walnuts,
   divided
¼ cup pure maple syrup

Lightly spoon the flour into a dry measuring cup to get a level measurement, then sift the flour into a large bowl. Add the farina (like Cream of Wheat), protein powder, Splenda®, baking soda, baking powder and salt to the sifted flour and mix well.

In a smaller bowl, combine the soy milk, applesauce and egg substitute and stir until well blended. Add the wet and dry mixes together, mix well, then let the batter stand for five minutes.

Coat a nonstick griddle or skillet with cooking spray and heat over medium heat. Pour about ¼ cup batter per pancake onto pan, then sprinkle each with 2 teaspoons walnuts. Cook 1 minute or until tops are covered with bubbles and edges look cooked. Carefully turn pancakes over, and cook 1 minute or until bottoms are lightly browned. Repeat procedure with remaining batter and walnuts. Serve with syrup. Serves 6.

To determine the category of golfer you fall into, we first look at the position of your pelvic bone. In perfect posture, the front ridge of your pelvic bone (ASIS or Anterior Superior Iliac Spine) should be only very slightly lower than the rear ridge of the bone (PSIS or Posterior Superior Iliac Spine). The belt line of someone with perfect posture (and no belly to distort the view), would look to be at about a 5-degree angle with the front lower than the back.

Next, we will look at any rotations and elevations of your posture. If you have ever heard someone say that their right leg is shorter than their left, chances are that unless they had an obvious birth defect and have been in treatment since the age of two, they actually have an elevated right hip. In other words, their legs are the exact same length, one just appears longer. Though they may say that they've "always" been like that, they can be changed, and we can help.

Low-Fat Whole Wheat Pancakes

1 cup and 2 tablespoons whole wheat pastry flour

1 tablespoon brown sugar

2 tablespoons apple sauce

1 scoop vanilla whey protein powder

1 cup and 2 tablespoons water

1 ½ teaspoons baking powder

Sift the flour into a large bowl. Add the brown sugar, protein powder and baking powder, and sift all four together again.

Add the apple sauce and water to the dry ingredients and mix until batter drips from spoon (but not too runny). If the batter seems too thick add more water.

Coat a non-stick griddle or skillet with cooking spray and heat over medium heat. Ladle about ¼ cup of batter into the pan and let it cook until small bubbles form in the center. Flip. Keep completed pancakes warm in a preheated oven covered with a paper towel to keep the moisture in.

Serve with a trans fat free margarine and maple syrup. For a special treat, make the batter with either ½ cup walnuts or ½ cup blueberries. Serves 4

Before choosing a style of grip, there some universal steps every grip follows:

First, for right handed golfers, place the club in your left hand with the end of the grip under the muscle pad of your palm, leaving one inch of the club extending beyond your hand. With your left index finger, hook the club shaft such that you can support the club under the muscle pad of your hand and your index finger.

Wrap the remaining fingers around the club shaft while placing the thumb slightly toward the right side of the club shaft. The V created between your right thumb and index finger should point toward your right shoulder.

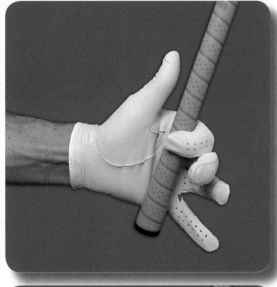

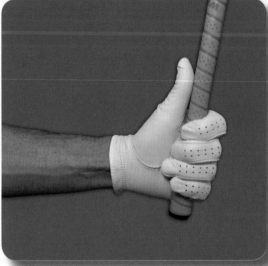

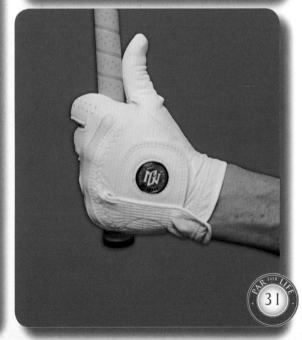

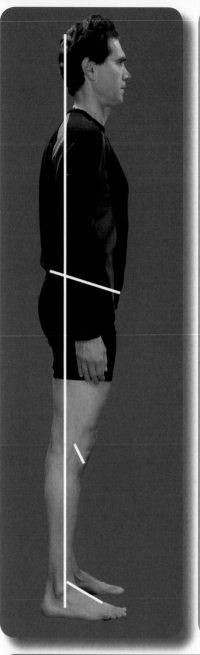

We call our first category of golfers IN THE ROUGH. The common denominator for this group is what is called an Anterior Pelvic Tilt, meaning the front of the pelvic bone is much lower than the rear.

This one deviation leads to many others. Often we see this condition coupled with a wide stance, feet everted (duck-feet), forward rounded shoulders and the head forward of the shoulders.

Posture deviations are not only an aesthetic issue, your body is designed to be in perfect alignment, and misalignments will cause pain. Our In the Rough Golfer will often have low back pain and tightness due to the lumbar spine being more compressed than designed. Hip and knee problems are prevalent. We all know this person, and often chalk up their aches and pains to their lifestyle, past or present. The truth is, however, our bodies are designed to continuously move and play through old age - activity in itself should not cause pain.

Stevia is a South American Herb that is sold in the United States as a dietary supplement. The herb is extremely sweet, and virtually calorie free. There is much debate within the FDA as to its use as a sweetener, but we have found it to be a good alternative to sugar. Cooking with Stevia can be tricky - it is so sweet that only a little is needed, and using too much can cause an aftertaste. For example, a batch of chocolate chip cookies only needs a half a teaspoon of Stevia instead of a cup or more of white sugar. Consider Stevia, and see if it is the sweetener for you.

Blueberry Waffles

3 eggs whites
1 cup low fat buttermilk
½ cup organic skim milk
1 tablespoon honey
¼ teaspoon vanilla extract
¾ cup whole wheat flour

¾ cup white flour or finely chopped oats
1 ½ teaspoon baking powder
½ teaspoon baking soda
½ teaspoon salt
½ pint blueberries

Preheat waffle iron on medium setting.

Blend egg whites, buttermilk, skim milk, honey and vanilla extract until smooth. Mix in flour baking powder, baking soda, salt and blueberries. Pour about one cup of batter into preheated, oiled waffle iron, leaving a little space around the edges. The batter will spread out to the edges when the top is closed.

Bake 10-12 minutes with out peeking. Top with more blueberries if desired. This is good topped with peanut butter and sliced bananas as well.

If you don't have buttermilk, place 1 teaspoon of apple cider vinegar in a 1 cup measuring cup and fill the rest of the way with low fat milk. Let stand for 5 minutes before adding to the recipe.

Fresh Strawberry Crepes

3 large eggs or egg substitute
   equivalent
5 large egg whites
¼ cup lowfat cottage cheese
3 tablespoons organic rolled oats

I scoop vanilla whey protein
   isolate powder
½ teaspoon vanilla extract
⅓ cup fresh or thawed, frozen
   strawberries (chopped)

Whip all ingredients except strawberries in blender. The batter should be very smooth.

Pour batter onto a preheated nonstick frying pan (coated with nonstick cooking spray) and cook until both sides are lightly browned. You will have about four 6-inch crepes.

Fill each crepe with ¼ of the strawberries and roll up.

Crepes can be filled with one or two teaspoons fat-free cream cheese, reduced-fat Neufchatel cheese, yogurt, or even cottage cheese. For a richer filling, blend the cheese or yogurt together with your favorite fruit. Chopped walnuts or almonds also taste great sprinkled on top. Makes 2 two crepe servings.

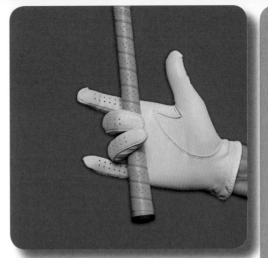

Next, with your right hand open and extended, place the club shaft vertically across the fingers between the palm and first knuckle of your middle fingers.

Wrap your remaining fingers around the shaft while placing the thumb slightly towards the left side of the club shaft. The V created between the right thumb and index finger should also point toward your right shoulder.

THE KNUCKLE CHECK
Check to make sure your knuckles are in alignment. We want to see the index finger of your left hand in line with the two middle fingers of your right hand. We call this the Knuckle Check, and will ask you to do this in each description of the grip styles. This quick & simple check will ensure that both hands are working together and not fighting against each other throughout your swing.

Our second group of golfers, OUT OF BOUNDS has their right and left sides of their body resting in different positions. One shoulder or hip may be higher or forward than the other. These elevations and rotations can be seen in only one or all of the four load joints. It is rare to see disparities in elevations between the right and left ankle or the right and left knee, but rotations like feet eversion or knee caps pointing off center are prevalent. We also find that one elevation or rotation can lead to the next - the body may compensate for a high right hip by also elevating the left shoulder. On the golf course, the Out of Bounds golfer tends to be inconsistent, sometimes overcoming their posture, and other times being overcome.

Eggs are a great source of protein... especially the whites. One large egg white delivers nearly 4 grams of protein. When choosing eggs, always look for free-range chickens who were fed an organic diet. Read the labels to ensure that you are buying the best product available.

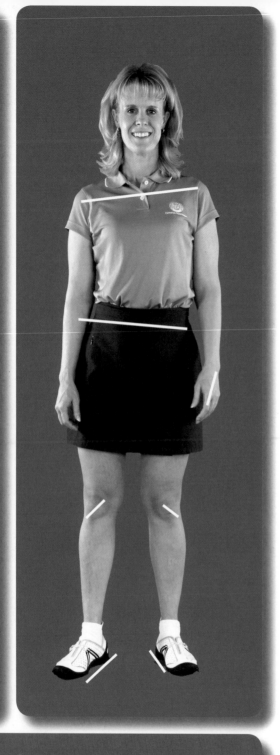

Mushroom & Herb Omelet

½ cup sliced fresh mushrooms
½ cup fat free egg substitute
¼ teaspoon dried chives
⅛ teaspoon dried dill

3 tablespoons shredded reduced-fat Swiss, or skim mozzarella cheese

Coat an 8-inch non-stick skillet with cooking spray, and preheat over medium heat. Add the mushrooms, cover, and cook for a couple of minutes, stirring occasionally, until the mushrooms are tender. Remove the mushrooms to a small dish, and cover to keep warm.

Respray the skillet, and return it to the heat. Add the egg substitute and sprinkle the herbs over the top. Reduce the heat to medium-low and cook without stirring for a couple of minutes, or until the omelet is set around the edges.

Use a spatula to lift the edges of the omelet, and allow the uncooked egg to flow below the cooked portion. Cook for another minute or two, or until the eggs are almost set.

Arrange first the mushrooms and then the cheese over half of the omelet. Fold the other half over the filling and cook for another minute or two, or until the cheese is melted and the eggs are completely set.

Slide omelet onto a plate, and serve hot.

Spanish Style Scrambled Eggs

1 teaspoon extra virgin olive oil
1 small ripe tomato, finely chopped
1 green onion, finely chopped
8 large egg whites
1 tablespoon salsa

Freshly ground pepper to taste
1 tablespoon minced fresh cilantro
Fresh cilantro or parsley sprigs
1 tomato, cut into wedges

In a large nonstick skillet, heat oil over medium-high heat. Add tomato and onion and sauté until the onion is soft, about 1 to 2 minutes. Reduce heat to low.

While the vegetables are cooking, in a bowl combine the egg, salsa, and pepper. Beat until frothy.

Pour the egg mixture over the tomatoes and onions into the skillet. Cook over low heat, stirring occasionally, until almost set. Add minced cilantro and stir until eggs are fully set. Garnish with cilantro sprigs and tomato. Serves 3

If you prefer an egg substitute to egg whites, use the equivalent liquid of six large eggs.

YOUR WRIST IS A HINGE

Another universal truth about grip - your wrist needs to act as a hinge in order to generate club head speed. Get comfortable with your grip while holding your club waist high, with your forearms parallel to the floor and your club pointing straight up at a 90° angle to the floor.

From this position, practice cocking your wrist up and down as if you were hammering a nail with both hands on the hammer. If you find you have difficulty hinging and un-hinging your wrists, grip the club more in your fingers. This should give you more flexibility. Being able to truly use your wrist as a hinge will allow your hands to release through the swing and increase your club head speed, giving you the ability to Tee it High & Let it Fly!

Don't ditch the garnish! Parsley is most widely used as a colorful garnish to decorate the plate. What isn't as widely known is that the bright herb is categorized in the flavanoid family and high in Vitamin C, folic acid and beta-carotene. It will also give you nice, fresh breath. It's one of the most alkalizing foods available as well. So clean your plate - of the garnish at least.

We talked about In the Rough golfers having an Anterior Pelvic Tilt. Our third group, NEED GREENS IN REGULATION is defined as having a posterior pelvic tilt. In this position, the rear crest of the pelvic bone is even with or lower than the front crest.

People who show a posterior pelvic tilt are on their way to changing the natural, gentle s-curve of their spine into a collapsed c-curve, if they are not there already. Though this posture is all too familiar in an elderly population, and we see it as a classic sign of the body aging, we also see this posture in many moms who are constantly carrying children on their hip, in very athletic bikers and pilates experts who are often in a state of flexion during their sport, and even in many long distance runners.

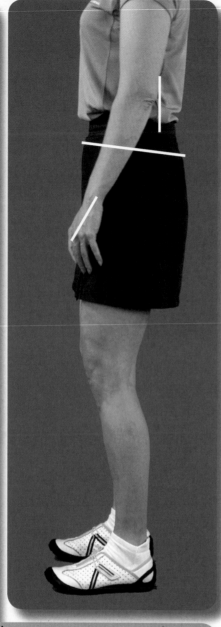

A posterior tilt may cause other compensations such as everted feet, flattening of the lower back, rounding of the upper back, and the head moving forward of the body to complete the c-curve.

Headaches and backaches are very typical in our Need Greens in Regulation golfers, but so are other aliments that are not intuitively connected to our posture. The biggest problem on the course that this group needs to overcome is that they are unable to maintain the proper hip and back position necessary to produce a consistent golf swing, which often leads to a lack of distance on the course.

Healthy Oatmeal

¾ cup water
¾ cup unsweetened apple cider
1 cup organic rolled oats
½ teaspoon salt (optional)
½ cup diced pear

¼ cup dried cranberries
½ teaspoon ground cinnamon
¼ teaspoon vanilla extract
¼ cup chopped pecans, toasted
¼ cup organic skim milk

Bring water and apple cider to a boil in a large saucepan. Stir in oats and salt; reduce heat to low, and cook for 3 minutes, stirring occasionally.

Add the pear, cranberries, cinnamon, and vanilla, stirring gently to combine; cook 3 minutes or until oats are tender. Stir in pecans and serve. A little extra water can be added for consistency, if needed. Serves 3

Committing to an annual blood test can save your life! It's one of the most important precautions you can take in extending your longevity. The results allow you to identify changes occurring in your body which can lead to disease, and many of these detrimental changes can be improved or reversed by modifying habits or adding nutritional supplements. Throughout this book we identify a number of tests we ask our Doctors to order, and suggest you should as well, including a CBC, complete hormone panel, homocystine, thyroid panel and C-Reactive Protein. If you can, begin with a baseline at age 25, and commit to an annual test every year after that.

Apricot Oat Muffins

1 cup rolled oats, plus additional for topping
1 cup whole wheat flour
$^1/_3$ cup packed brown sugar - Splenda® blend
2 teaspoons milled organic flax seeds
$^1/_3$ cup wheat germ
2 teaspoons baking powder
1$^1/_2$ teaspoons grated orange zest
1 teaspoon ground cinnamon
$^1/_2$ teaspoon salt
2 lightly beaten egg whites
1 cup organic skim milk
$^1/_4$ cup expeller pressed canola oil
$^3/_4$ cup sliced almonds (raw and non-salted)
$^1/_4$ cup low sugar apricot fruit spread, plus additional for glaze

Preheat oven to 400°. Generously coat muffin tins with nonstick cooking spray. This recipe fills either 12 regular sized muffins, 6 jumbo sized muffins, or 18 muffin tops. We recommend the tops.

In a large bowl, mix together all of the dry ingredients and the orange zest. In a smaller bowl, mix the remaining ingredients together except for the apricot spread and mix well.

Add the wet ingredients to the dry ingredients all at once and mix until just blended. The batter should be a little thin.

Fill each muffin cup about $^1/_3$ full. Carefully spoon 1 teaspoon of the apricot spread onto each muffin. Spoon the remaining batter on top of the fruit spread. Sprinkle each muffin with oats.

Bake for 20 to 22 minutes until golden brown. Remove from the oven and place on a wire rack. Lightly brush each muffin with some apricot spread. Let stand for 10 minutes. Remove from pan and serve warm.

This recipe lends itself well to using almost any flavor of fruit. Try raspberry jam and replace the orange zest with the same amount of lemon zest, or blueberry preserves and replace the orange zest with 1$^1/_2$ tsp of pure almond extract.

Don't Wait... PRACTICE IN THE KITCHEN!
Golf is a pervasive part of your life. No need to fight it - golf away! When you're in the kitchen or at the grill, use whatever utensil you have to practice your grip. The pressure in your hands should always be firm yet supple. Check your knuckles, and make sure that your "clubface" faces the target.
You should become very comfortable with the idea that your grip will directly influence the position of your clubface at address and impact.
One word of caution in the kitchen - don't swing too big – we cannot be held responsible for any food flung on the ceiling!

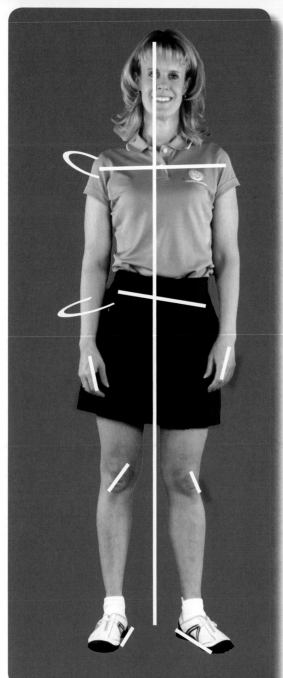

Though we place golfers into one of three simple groups, many times we find that people show deviations of the Out of Bounds, rotations and elevations, as well as either an In The Rough or a Need Greens in Regulation golfer. Of course, since last two mentioned categories are defined by the position of the pelvic bone, we cannot have a combination of these positions.

When we combine elevations and rotations with an anterior or posterior pelvic tilt, the possibilities of postural deviations become seemingly endless, especially when we further complicate the matter by adding differing severities of each misalignment.

To illustrate our posture examples we have "faked" positions (especially an ideal posture!). Though looking at the same person displaying different conditions may look exaggerated, the truth is, these pictures truly show how everyday people look. If you don't believe our photos, take one of yourself or one of a friend head-on and how you normally stand. You may be shocked at what a critical eye will tell you about your own posture.

Low-Fat Blueberry Muffins

1 $\frac{1}{4}$ cups whole wheat flour
$\frac{1}{2}$ cup wheat germ
$\frac{1}{2}$ cup rolled oats
$\frac{1}{4}$ cup unsweetened shredded coconut
$\frac{1}{2}$ cup Splenda®
1 $\frac{1}{2}$ teaspoons baking powder
$\frac{1}{2}$ teaspoon salt
1 $\frac{1}{2}$ cup fresh blueberries, rinsed and drained

$\frac{3}{4}$ cup organic skim milk
$\frac{1}{4}$ cup egg substitute
$\frac{1}{3}$ cup applesauce
3 egg whites, whipped to soft peaks
$\frac{1}{4}$ rolled oats
2 tablespoons unsweetened shredded coconut
2 tablespoons brown sugar-Splenda® blend

Preheat oven to 400°. Spray either 12 regular sized muffin cups, 6 jumbo muffin cups, or 18 muffin tops with non-stick cooking spray.

Sift the flour into a large mixing bowl. In a food processor, chop the oats and the $\frac{1}{4}$ cup of coconut together into as fine as a grain as you can, then add it to the flour along with the Splenda®, baking powder & salt.

In a smaller bowl, whip the egg whites into soft peaks, then gently fold in the milk, egg substitute and applesauce.

Add the wet mixture to the dry and mix together just until combined. Gently add in the blueberries. Pour into the muffin pan.

In a food processor, chop the remaining oats, coconut and brown sugar blend together well. Sprinkle on top of each muffin before baking. Bake at 400° for 25 minutes.

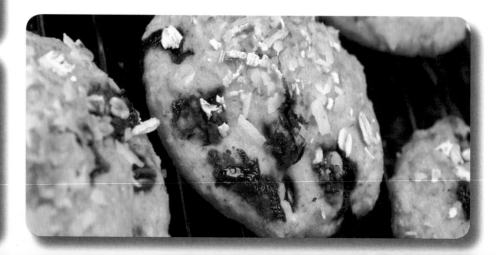

Crunchy Protein Granola

2 cups rolled oats
½ cup oat bran
1 scoop vanilla whey protein
  isolate powder
¼ teaspoon salt
½ cup sunflower seeds
½ cup chopped nuts - sliced raw,
  unsalted almonds work well
1 teaspoon cinnamon

1 tablespoon milled organic
  flax seeds
⅓ cup canola oil
¼ cup honey or maple syrup
½ tablespoon vanilla extract
¼ cup brown sugar, packed
½ cup pumpkin seeds
½ cup mixed dried berries

Preheat the oven to 325°. Spray a 13x18" baking tray with nonstick spray.

Combine the oats, oat bran, protein powder, salt, sunflower seeds, nuts, cinnamon and flax seeds in a large bowl.

Combine the oil, honey, and vanilla; pour this mixture into the bowl of dry mix. Mix thoroughly (use your hands if necessary). Transfer the mixture to the prepared tray, and spread it out.

Bake for 35-45 minutes, or until golden, stirring once or twice during the baking.

Put the granola in a large bowl, crumble in the sugar and let it melt in. Stir in the pumpkin seeds and dried fruit and then return it to the tray to cool. Let it cool completely. Once it's completely cool, then it will be crunchy. Makes 8 generous servings.

Use this Granola for a Great Cereal:
4 to 6 ounces of Plain or Vanilla Oraganic, Cultured Yogurt
Serving of Granola
1 Scoop of Whey Protein Isolate Powder
½ cup Fresh Blueberries or other Fruit
1 tablespoon Flaxseed Oil

Keeping your blood sugar at a low, constant level is critical to everyone's long term health, not just to diabetics who are forced to focus on the issue. Consuming high fiber foods can help you avoid insulin spikes. Fiber is digested slowly, which may help to slow the absorption of sugar in your body. Fiber has also been shown to lower cholesterol and help to control weight gain. To get these benefits, along with the obvious benefits of fiber, try to get 30-35 grams per day.

Though every person may have a very different list of postural deviations, we always find one common element - most "unavoidable" aches and pains of aging are due to these misalignments, and thus can be reduced or eliminated if we can get the joints of the body back into a more proper alignment.

No matter what golfer category you fall into, our hope is that you will find help in this book and through the Par For Life Institute. Our goal is to give golfers the tools to get their bodies into a more proper alignment, which will not only relieve their aches and pains, but be better able to perform a proper golf swing and improve their game. This combination will allow you to play as much golf as you want for as long as you like,

As you read down the left side of this book, you will find exercises and tips designed to realign your joints and strengthen your body in order to keep them that way. The series of exercises, we call it a recipe, is a very general workout. For best results, we suggest that you consult the Par For Life Institute to address your personal postural deviations and fitness goals. Enjoy the exercises, and we hope that they serve you as they do us - as an invaluable tool to increase the longevity of your golf game.

Easy Coffee Cake

²/₃ cup whole wheat pastry flour
½ cup all purpose flour
I teaspoon baking soda
I teaspoon ground cinnamon
I ½ cups finely chopped, peeled apples
¼ cup egg substitute
³/₄ cup Splenda®
¼ cup chopped walnuts or pecans

¼ cup applesauce
¼ cup packed brown sugar
I tablespoon whole wheat flour
I tablespoon all purpose flour
½ teaspoon cinnamon
I tablespoon trans fat free margarine
¼ cup chopped walnuts or pecans

Preheat oven to 350°. Lightly coat a 9-inch round baking pan with nonstick cooking spray; set aside. In a small bowl combine whole wheat flour, all-purpose flour, baking soda, and cinnamon; set aside. In a large bowl toss together the apple and egg substitute. Stir in the Splenda®, walnuts, and applesauce. Add flour mixture; stir just until combined. Pour batter onto the prepared pan.

In a small bowl stir together ¼ cup packed brown sugar, I tablespoon whole wheat flour, I tablespoon all-purpose flour, and ½ teaspoon ground cinnamon; cut in I tablespoon trans fat free margarine until crumbly. Stir in ¼ cup chopped walnuts or pecans. Sprinkle this crumb topping over batter.

Bake for 30 to 35 minutes or until toothpick inserted near the center comes out clean. Cool coffeecake in pan about 10 minutes. Serve warm. Makes 10 servings.

When you get an annual blood test, you should always get the basic CBC. Short for Chemistry Panel and Complete Blood Count, the CBC provides information assessing cardiovascular health, kidney function, liver function, blood protein levels, red and white cell profiles, and blood mineral levels. It's the first test doctors normally order, and covers many key functions in the body. When you are looking to maximize your longevity, however, don't let your doctor's analysis stop with this test.

Before completing our discussion on grip, we, of course, need to illustrate the three most common grips. The grip you choose will largely depend on what feels comfortable for you and gives you the best reults. Some golfers even choose to change the type of grip they use depending on the shot. Whichever you choose, always make sure that your knuckles are lined up correctly, your pressure is firm, yet supple and that you are able to cock your wrist forward and back like a hinge.

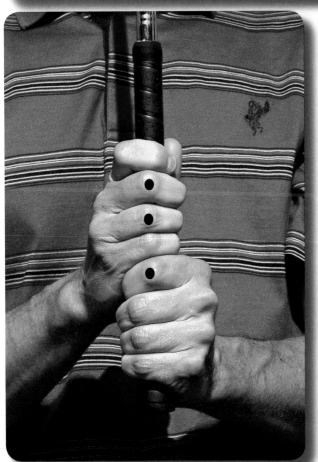 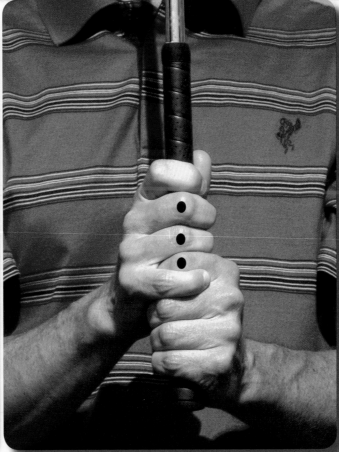 

THE 10 FINGER GRIP
A comfortable grip for the beginner, the Ten Finger Grip very simply puts all ten fingers on the Club. We find that this grip aids in power and tends to work well for women and juniors. If this is the grip for you, make sure that all of your knuckles are in alignment, and keep your pressure firm and supple.

THE OVERLAP GRIP
The overlap grip is probably the most popular grip taught by golf instructors, and the greatest number of people enjoy success with this grip. While we offer grip tips, to ensure yours is the one for you, it really is best to consult with a PGA Professional, preferably one who takes into account your personal body structure.
This grip will aid you in keeping a balanced address position, setting you up for a better swing.

INTERLOCK GRIP
The Interlock grip may not be as popular as the Overlap, but certainly is used by some of the greatest golfers who have ever graced the course - Jack Nicklaus, for one.
Not only does Mr. Nicklaus feel comfortable with this grip, he finds this is his best position to have both hands working as one unit.

The Hunt Club Restaurant
Geneva National Golf Club, Lake Geneva, Wisconsin

Soups, Salad & Set-Up

Soups & Salads are a staple at the Par For Life Institute. Our perfect lunch is a big salad full of a variety of fresh, organic vegetables with grilled fish or chicken and a great tasting, healthy dressing. On some days, however, nothing hits the spot like a warm bowl of soup, which is also a great way to get more vegetables in your diet.

Most at-home salads are simple - grab the veggies out of the fridge, throw them together and toss it with dressing. Nine out of ten times that's absolutely perfect and helps you get your necessary daily servings of vegetables.

When you have time to make something new, or are entertaining and need suggestions, turn to the pages from Par For Life. Look for the make ahead tips on some of the recipes. We know you - you're looking to spend more time on the golf course than in the kitchen, and we couldn't be happier about that!

Salads are a staple in your diet, and your set-up is essential for your golf game! In this chapter we will discuss how you address the ball in the best way possible to use your body's natural design and be able to make Par For Life!

Palmer #17
Geneva National Golf Club
Lake Geneva, Wisconsin

In the breakfast section we discussed how we look at posture. Now we will start to show you how we use simple stretches and exercises, both on and off the golf course, that serve to realign our joints and remind our muscles to put our bones back into a more proper posture.

Patience is a virtue, in more way than one. When starting on this general Par For Life exercise program or one designed specifically for you through our Institute, your goal should be to eliminate aches and pains and get your body into a functional, proper position that will allow you to play as much golf as you want for as long as you like.

Many people feel immediate results, but keep in mind that a permanent transformation takes time, maybe even years. You may experience temporary "new" aches as we re-engage dormant muscles and make them move again as they should. Just remember, if you are like 99.9% of us, your body has made compensations for its improper position for years, and it takes time to reverse that. The good news - it can be reversed!

Fresh Crab with Mustard

1 bag (5 ounces) mixed lettuces, shredded	2 tablespoons Dijon mustard
	2 tablespoons white wine vinegar
3 tablespoons fresh chopped chives	1 tablespoon flax seed oil
	4 tablespoons extra virgin olive oil
2 cups fresh cooked crab meat	Salt and black pepper to taste

For the dressing, mix together the mustard, vinegar, flax seed oil, olive oil and salt and pepper in a blender or with a hand mixer. If you have time to refrigerate for one hour prior to serving, that is preferred, but the dressing may also be used fresh.

Take the cooled crab meat and chop or shred into smaller pieces. Toss the crab with a small amount of the dressing, just enough to coat the meat.

Toss the salad with the dressing so that all leaves are lightly coated. Divide the salad on to four plates. Top each plate with an equal amount of crab, and sprinkle the chives over each plate.   Serves 4

Tomato, Onion & Feta Salad

4 large tomatoes, thinly sliced
1 red onion, thinly sliced
Salt and pepper to taste
2 tablespoons chopped fresh basil
3 oz reduced fat feta, crumbled

3 tablespoons organic, low-fat
  plain yogurt
2 tablespoons extra virgin
  olive oil
1 tablespoon white wine vinegar

Arrange the tomato and onion slices on a large serving plate and season with salt and pepper.

Blend the feta, yogurt, oil and vinegar until smooth in a food processor or using a hand blender. Drizzle the mixture over the tomatoes, then sprinkle with basil. Serves 6

Set-up in golf is no different than in other areas in life - a good beginning gets you good results. As we talk about the proper address position, we go back to our discussion on the ideal posture position. At address, you should strive to keep your shoulders, hips, knees and ankles level with the ground and with each other. This is where you may hear PGA Professionals attacking our philosophy. Often, Pros will ask you to add excessive tilt to your torso, saying that since your right hand is lower, you need to tilt to the right. DON'T DO IT. Like the late, great Sam Snead said, keep your lines straight!

Tomatoes have been in the news in the last ten years touting their delivery of Lycopene. Lycopene is an antioxidant that may help in the prevention of cancer (prostate cancer in particular), and also in the prevention of heart disease by lowering LDL's and blood pressure. Cooking tomatoes serves to release more Lycopene than eating raw tomatoes, so, if you are looking to find the greatest amount of Lycopene, look to freshly made soups and sauces.

Avocado & Chicken Salad

1 tablespoon lemon juice
½ teaspoon Tabasco® sauce
2 teaspoon chopped oregano
⅓ cup extra virgin olive oil
½ cup finely chopped red onion
4 half chicken breasts, skinless and boneless
1 tablespoon extra virgin olive oil
Salt and black pepper

½ cup black olives, pitted and halved
½ cup chopped fresh mint leaves
3 tablespoons chopped fresh parsley
6-8 sun dried tomatoes, quartered
2 firm ripe avocados
About 16 leaves of butter-head or other soft-leafed lettuce

To make the dressing whisk together the lemon juice, Tabasco® sauce and 1 teaspoon of oregano. Add the extra virgin olive oil in a stream, whisking until the dressing is emulsified. Stir in the onion.

Heat a well-seasoned ribbed grill pan over moderately high heat. Pat the chicken dry and rub with oregano, salt and pepper. Grill chicken 5 to 7 minutes. Turn and grill another 5 to 7 minutes, or until cooked through.

Transfer the chicken to a plate and let it cool to room temperature. Cut the chicken into slices and pour most of the dressing over it to marinade for about 15 minutes, stirring occasionally.

Toss the olives, mint, parsley and tomatoes and with the salad leaves well. Divide the greens onto six salad plates. Slice the avocados, place equal amounts of avocado and chicken on each plate and serve.

PAR FOR LIFE EXERCISE RECIPE 1

For best results, perform this series daily, preferably in the morning in order to get your body in a better alignment for the remainder of the day.

1 - Arm Circles. 40 repetitions front and back

2- Shoulder Rolls. 40 repetitions front and back

3 - Counter Stretch. Hold for one minute

4 - Static Extension. Hold for one minute

5 - Sitting Twist. Hold for one minute on each side

6 - IT Band Stretch. Hold for one minute on each side.

7 - Cats & Dogs. 10 of each, alternating.

8 - Gravity Drop. Hold for one minute.

Throughout the Soup & Salad section you will find photos and explanations of each of these exercises. For further instruction, visit www.ParForLife.com.

Avocados are full of "Good Fats." We place so much emphasis today on being low or no fat, but the truth is that our bodies do need fats, and avocados are a great, healthy source. Though they are a high fat food, with 25 grams of fat in one medium sized avocado, the same fruit will also deliver 12 grams of fiber and 1 gram of protein. Avocados also have more potassium than a banana, and contain more Vitamin E than any other fruit.

Black Bean Soup

2 teaspoons extra virgin olive oil
2 teaspoons minced garlic
1 cup chopped onions
1 cup chopped carrots
1 can (19 oz) organic black beans, drained (or 12 oz cooked beans)

3 cups organic, fat-free chicken broth
¾ teaspoons ground cumin
¼ cup chopped cilantro

Add the oil to a nonstick saucepan and heat over a medium flame. Add the garlic, onions and carrots and cook, stirring occasionally, for 4 minutes or until the onion is softened.

Add beans, chicken stock and cumin to the onions and bring to a boil. Cover, reduce heat to medium low and simmer for 20 minutes or until carrots are softened. Transfer to food processor and puree until smooth. Ladle into bowls and sprinkle with cilantro

Prepare and refrigerate up to a day ahead and reheat gently before serving, adding more stock if too thick   Serves 4

When you address the ball and we look at you from the front view, we should be able to draw parallel lines to the ground straight through both knees, both hips and both shoulders. Just as we are designed to display these straight lines when standing, we need to maintain them as we bend over a golf ball.

From the side, when standing, we should still see the natural s-curve of the spine when you tilt from the hips. The knees break slightly, and the shoulders are back and relaxed, not reaching for the ball. Keep your eye on the curve - it is what allows us to move and gives us balance unlike any other creature on earth. Too many golfers show a rounded back at address, which greatly limits their mobility through the swing.

Fresh Tomato Soup with Guacamole

¼ teaspoon ground cumin

2 pounds tomatoes (about 4 large ones), peeled, seeded, and chopped

1 onion, coarsley chopped

3 tablespoons minced jalapeno pepper

1 tablespoon uncooked brown rice

2 cups water

½ teaspoon Splenda®

Salt and pepper to taste

½ small ripe avocado

1 chopped scallion including green top

2 tablespoons chopped cilantro, plus whole leaves for serving

1 teaspoon lime juice

In a medium pot, combine the tomatoes, onion, 1 tablespoon of the jalapeno, the rice, and ground cumin. Cover the pot and bring to a simmer over moderate heat. Reduce the heat and cook, stirring occasionally, until the rice is very soft, about 30 minutes.

Puree the tomato mix in a blender or food processor until smooth. Return the puree to the pot and stir in the water. Add the Splenda® and season with salt and pepper to your liking. Bring the soup just to a simmer over moderate heat.

In a small bowl, mash the avocado with a fork. Stir in the scallion, chopped cilantro, lime juice, and remaining 2 tablespoons jalapeno. Season with salt and pepper.

Ladle the soup into four bowls and top with the guacamole. Scatter the cilantro leaves over all. Serves 4

ARM CIRCLES

Stand with your feet directly under your hips and your quadriceps held tight. Bend your fingertips to your palms and lock your thumb straight. Pinch your shoulder blades together and lift your arms up to shoulder height, parallel with the floor and palms down. Holding your quads tight and keeping your lower body stable, circle your arms forward for forty repetitions. Roll your arms back with your thumbs pointed backward and your palms up, and circle backward for forty repetitions. This exercise serves to open up your chest and shoulders, creating a functional extension through your entire spine.

Cilantro Chili Chicken Salad

3 quarts water
2 1/2 pounds boneless & skinless
   chicken breasts
1 large bunch of fresh, cilantro,
   finely chopped
4 large garlic cloves, finely
   minced
1 tablespoon of fresh ginger,
   peeled & minced, about 1 1/2
   inches

2 fresh jalapeno peppers, seeded
   & finely minced
1/2 teaspoon of kosher salt
Juice of 1 1/2 large lemons
1/3 cup flax seed oil

3 cups thinly sliced celery or bok
   choy
1/2 cup thinly sliced green onion

Start the chicken early (you can even cook it the day before). Bring the water and chicken to a big boil. Turn the heat off and let cool to room temperature before draining. This is a great way to prepare chicken for any cold recipe.

While the chicken is cooling, blend the cilantro, garlic, ginger, jalapeno, salt, lemon juice and flax seed oil together into a smooth vinaigrette. Let sit at room temperature until the chicken is cool.

Once cooled, chop the chicken into comfortable cubes and mix with the vinaigrette mixture, celery or bok choy and green onion. Serve on top of a salad or as a sandwich or wrap.

The "ready" position in golf is similar to most other sports, so relate the position of your upper body tilt to a sport you may have played before. Bend your knees slightly, and tilt from your hips, keeping your s-curve in tact. Can you do this? If so, Congratulations! If not, you will get there - refer to your body condition and exercise recipes. You can and will achieve a more proper alignment and restore function in your body.

Garlic is in the news so often for its benefits, you may think it's a Super Food! We caution you always to never buy into an idea that one food or one supplement will cure all of your ills, but do an internet search on garlic right now, and you can find numerous studies proving its benefits on lowering blood pressure and cholesterol, and offering up the bulb to assist your body with its antibacterial and antifungal properties. The list goes on and on, but the conclusion is this - Garlic is a great food - tasty and healthy. All you need to worry about are the mints!

Classic Caesar Salad

1 egg, separated
2 cloves of garlic, finely chopped
2½ tablespoons fresh squeezed lemon juice
⅛ cup extra virgin olive oil
⅛ cup organic flax seed oil
2 tablespoons organic apple cider vinegar

½ teaspoon salt
½ teaspoon Worcestershire Sauce
¼ teaspoon black pepper
1 large head romaine lettuce
Fresh shaved parmesan cheese
Flat anchovies (optional)

In a blender, combine the egg yolk, garlic, lemon juice, olive oil, flax seed oil, apple cider vinegar, salt, pepper and Worcestershire sauce. Mix for one minute until well blended. Add the egg white and mix well. Dressing can be made ahead and chilled for up to three hours or used immediately.

Chop the lettuce into 1 inch strips across the spine. Chop the anchovies into large pieces, and add the anchovies and cheese to the lettuce. Place in a large serving bowl and toss with the dressing immediately before serving.

SHOULDER ROLLS

Stand with your feet directly under your hips and your toes pointed forward. Tighten your quadriceps, and take care to keep your lower body perfectly still throughout the exercise. With big motions, roll your shoulders in forward circles for forty repetitions. Reverse the motion and roll the shoulders backward forty times. Throughout the exercise, work to get a full range of motion in the shoulders and the scapular area.

At the Par for Life institute we believe that when you are engaged in exercise and sport activity, it is essential to keep your spine in alignment. Many of our students work with a chiropractor who also is a certified clinical kinesiologist. We have found this combination to produce the best, long lasting results. Their anatomical and biological understanding of the body translates to solutions for many of your health challenges.

Cranberry Chicken Salad

2 pounds boneless and skinless chicken breasts

1 cup reduced fat canola mayonnaise

$^1/_2$ cup chopped celery

$^1/_2$ cup dried cranberries

$^1/_4$ cup chopped green onions

Cook and cube the chicken breasts. A great way to prepare chicken for a cold salad is to place it covered in water in a large pot, bring it to a boil, and then remove from heat and let cool, still in the water.

In a large bowl, mix the chicken, mayonnaise, celery, cranberries & onions together. Serve as a sandwich, in a pita or by itself on a bed of greens.

Even Distribution

Weight on the Right

One important component of a successful golf swing is the ability to effectively transfer your weight back and through the swing. In order to do this consistently, begin with your weight distributed **evenly** on both your right and left sides. Some pros may ask you to start with your weight more on one leg. If you'd like consistency in your game, don't listen to them!

Our bodies are designed for bilateral function, that is, both sides working identically. Starting your address with your weight on one side interferes with our natural design, and when we defy our design, we are destined for failure! For a consistent game, start with your weight even left to right.

Almond Chicken Salad

2 large chicken breasts, boneless and skinless
2 quarts water
1/2 cup dried apricots, cut into quarters
1/4 cup whole, raw, unsalted almonds

1 small celery stalk, chopped
1/2 cup fat free plain yogurt
2 tablespoons chopped fresh cilantro
1 tablespoon Dijon mustard
1 tablespoon orange zest
1 tablespoon organic honey

Place water and chicken into a large sauce pan and bring to a boil. Turn off heat and let cool completely in the water.

Pat the chicken dry and dice into cubes. Mix all ingredients together well and chill for one hour before serving.

Almonds are another great food with numerous benefits attributed to them. Clinical studies have shown almonds to help reduce LDL cholesterol and maintain a healthy body weight. As do most nuts, almonds deliver a good source of the right fats. Choose raw & un-salted - they make a great snack food in your desk drawer!

COUNTER STRETCH

In this exercise, we are working to stretch your shoulders and upper back, while keeping your lower back in a functional and proper s-curve as you bend from the hips.

Place your hands on the edge of a counter - a high counter is less difficult than a waist-high counter. Step your feet back and bend forward from the waist until you can fully extend your arms and back. As you hold this stretch for one minute, work on lengthening your spine. Your shoulder blades are collapsed together, but the tops of your shoulders should be relaxed and down. Concentrate on rolling your hips forward so that you continue to create a proper s-curve in your low back.

Cilantro Shrimp Salad

3 cups cooked shrimp, peeled and deveined

⅓ cup red onion, finely chopped

¼ cup green bell pepper, finely chopped

¼ cup red bell pepper, finely chopped

¼ cup orange or yellow bell pepper, finely chopped

⅓ cup fresh cilantro, finely chopped

2 tablespoons extra virgin olive oil

1 tablespoon lime juice

¼ teaspoon ground black pepper

Combine the shrimp, onions, peppers, and cilantro in a medium bowl and toss to mix. Drizzle with the olive oil and lime juice, sprinkle with the pepper and toss again to mix well. Chill for at least one hour before serving. Serves 4.

Even Distribution

Weight Forward

Weight Back

From the side view, we also want your weight to be even on your feet, toes to heels. Again, we are going against the grain of some teaching Pros. Often golf instructors tell students to have their weight more on their heels. Golf is a sport, and try walking, running or jumping in any other sport with this weight distribution - it's impossible!

Good posture at the address position gives you the same advantage as in any other sport. Your body is springy with live tension in it. Keep your weight squarely in the center of your stance, and you're ready for action.

Chilled Edamame Salad

1 tablespoon rice wine vinegar	2 tablespoons minced scallions
1 teaspoon canola oil	2 tablespoons finely chopped
1 teaspoon lemon juice	celery
2 teaspoons organic honey	1 large radish, finely chopped
$1/8$ teaspoon black pepper	$1/4$ cup finely chopped cucumber
$1/2$ cup cooked edamame, shelled	

In small bowl, whisk vinegar, oil, lemon juice, honey, and pepper. Place remaining ingredients in large bowl and toss with vinegar mixture. Chill 30 minutes.

GOLF CART STRETCH

We will take a moment to divert from our recipe to add an exercise modification for the golf course. Stretching during a round of golf is essential to keeping your body loose and able to keep swinging in rhythm and pain free.

The counter stretch on page 52 is a great stretch for your back. Since you won't find too many counters on the course (though stretching at the snack bar is allowed), the roof of your golf car makes the perfect prop. Place your hands on top of the cart, bend from your waist and stretch your back all the way through your shoulders.

Do this often throughout your round. The golf swing works your spine from side to side, so it needs to be stretched front to back!

Black Bean Chili

1 tablespoon extra virgin olive oil
1 large onion, chopped (1 cup)
1 medium zucchini or yellow
   squash, chopped (1½ cups)
1 medium green bell pepper,
   chopped (1 cup)
1 medium red bell pepper,
   chopped (1 cup)
1½ teaspoons ground cumin
1½ teaspoons chili powder
½ teaspoon dried basil

3 cans (16 ounce) organic
   black beans
⅔ cup picante sauce or salsa
1 large can (28 ounces) diced
   tomatoes
Salt and pepper, to taste
Non-fat plain yogurt
Grated, reduced fat cheddar
   cheese
Fresh minced cilantro

Heat the oil over medium heat in a soup pot. Peel and coarsely chop the onion, adding it to the pot as you chop. Cook, stirring from time to time, while you cut the zucchini into bite size pieces, adding them to the pot as you cut. Raise the heat to medium-high. Seed the green and red bell peppers, and cut them into small pieces, adding them to the pot as you cut. Cook the vegetables, stirring from time to time, until they are tender, about 5 to 7 minutes more.

While the vegetables cook, add the cumin, chili powder and basil. Stir well. Rinse the black beans in colander and set aside to drain. When the vegetables are tender, add picante sauce and tomatoes and juices. Stir well. Cook, uncovered, 3 minutes, stirring occasionally.

Add the drained black beans and stir them into the mixture very gently so as not to break up the beans. Bring the mixture to a moderate boil, then reduce the heat to medium-low to maintain the slow boil. Allow the chili to cook, uncovered, until the beans are heated through, about 5 minutes more.

Remove chili from the heat, or simmer until ready to serve. To serve, ladle the chili into bowls and garnish each serving, if desired, with yogurt, cheese and cilantro.

We all know that men and women are made differently, and, in our opinion, ladies have the design advantage when it comes to the golf swing. Due to the mechanics of child bearing, a woman's hips are slightly wider than a man's, making the angle which the female's femur inserts into the hip socket distinctively different than a man.

Due to this inherent difference in our hip positions, women tend to have greater flexibility through their hips and lower back, and thus often have an easier time at achieving a proper pelvic tilt.

That being said, take heart, men. Getting into the proper address position is only part of the equation, and there tends to be no other functional differences between the sexes.

Keep your knees slightly flexed, tilt from your hips, and maintain the natural s-curve in your spine.

Grilled Romaine Salad

2 whole hearts of romaine
    lettuce heads
Extra virgin olive oil
Balsamic vinegar

1 clove garlic, crushed
1 tablespoon light canola
    mayonnaise
1 tablespoon Dijon mustard
Fresh grated parmesan cheese

¼ cup extra virgin olive oil
¼ cup white wine vinegar

Make the dressing ahead of time by combining olive oil, white wine vinegar, garlic, mayonnaise, and mustard and mixing well in a blender or with a whisk. Refrigerate for one hour or more.

Cut the hearts of romaine in half, lengthwise. Lightly brush the cut side with olive oil and balsamic vinegar. Grill, cut side down, for about 4 minutes. Top grilled romaine hearts with dressing & parmesan cheese, and serve immediately. Serves 4.

STATIC EXTENSION

Get on your hands and knees with your knees directly under your hips and your hands directly under your shoulders. Walk your hands forward about 8 inches, and shift your weight forward so that your shoulders are directly over your hands and your hips are forward of your knees. Make sure you keep your behind up. Hold this position with your elbows locked straight, bow your head slightly down and collapse your shoulders and your low back. Hold this position for one minute.

This exercise promotes proper extension throughout your spine, especially in your shoulders, making you better able to hold them back in a neutral position throughout your swing. This exercise is great for any type of functional body. However, if you display an anterior pelvic tilt and are experiencing low back pain, you may want to go easy on this one until your pain is under control.

Light Chicken Caesar Salad

1 large head of romaine lettuce, outer leaves and core removed

2 cooked chicken breast fillets, cut into 1 ¼ inch cubes

2 tablespoons finely chopped flat-leaf parsley

⅓ cup freshly shredded parmesan cheese

3 thick slices of whole grain bread

½ cup low-fat plain yogurt

3 tablespoons light canola mayonnaise

2 tablespoons Dijon mustard

1 tablespoon lemon juice

¼ teaspoon Worcestershire sauce

1-2 cloves crushed garlic

Preheat the oven to 350°. Remove the crusts from the bread and cut into ¼ inch cubes. Place on a tray. Bake for 12 minutes, or until lightly browned. Turn once to brown evenly. Set aside to cool and crisp.

Meanwhile combine the yogurt, mayonnaise, mustard, lemon juice, and Worcestershire sauce in a bowl, adding the garlic to taste. Season with black pepper.

Break the lettuce leaves into smaller pieces in a large serving bowl. Add the chicken, bread, parsley and parmesan. Toss through with two-thirds of the dressing. Divide in servings and scatter the remaining parsley, parmesan and remaining dressing. Serve with crusty bread.

Mobile & Stable   Stable, Not Mobile

MOBILITY & STABILITY

At first glance, these two states seem to be at odds. However, to achieve our best golf game, or our best in any sport, we need to have the best of both worlds and be mobile and stable simultaneously. Mobility allows us to transfer weight easily through the swing, and stability gives us the ability to create the power we need. Who wouldn't want both?

For most body conditions, the best way to achieve both of these attributes through your golf swing is to keep your feet no greater than shoulder width apart. Sam Snead advocated this address position. When he wanted to hit it hard, he made sure his feet were right underneath him...and boy, could he hit it! Judging by his performance on the tee well into his nineties, Mr. Snead certainly achieved our common goal, to make Par For Life!

To achieve the greatest amount of mobility and stability, keep your feet no wider than shoulder width apart.

SITTING TWIST

A golfer's favorite. Sit with your legs extended in front of you, quadriceps tight and roll your pelvis forward to sit very straight up. Place your right foot on the outside of your left knee. Keeping your left quad tight and your back very straight, twist your torso to the right, looking over your right shoulder. Hold for one minute, continually challenging yourself to stay very upright through the twist, and making sure your weight is even throughout both hips. Repeat on the left side.

Apple Spinach Salad

2 cups baby spinach leaves
1 medium apple, thinly sliced
   (crisp & tart works best)
2 tablespoons chopped celery
2 tablespoons raw organic
   pecans

$^1/_2$ cup apple cider vinegar
2 tablespoons extra
   virgin olive oil
Salt & black pepper to taste

Whisk the vinegar, olive oil, salt and pepper together to make the dressing. Place in a sealed container and refrigerate.

Preheat the oven to 350°. Chop the pecans and spread in a single layer in shallow baking pan. Bake for 8-10 minutes or until lightly toasted, stirring occasionally.

In a large salad bowl, toss the spinach, apples, celery and pecans together with the dressing and serve immediately. Serves 4.

Making any salad a meal is a great way to get your vegetables and protein in your diet without over-doing the carbs. Take this Apple Spinach Salad, for example. Add some grilled chicken breast strips, even from the night before, and you have a quick, tasty and healthy meal.

Mixed Greens with Parmesan Crisps

1 cup grated parmesan cheese

2 teaspoons finely chopped fresh
    rosemary

4 cups mixed baby salad greens

½ cup seedless red grapes,
    halved

½ cup walnut pieces

⅓ cup red wine vinegar

1 garlic clove, coarsely chopped

2 tablespoons coarsely chopped
    shallots

½ teaspoon salt (optional)

½ teaspoon dried oregano

½ teaspoon dried basil

½ teaspoon coarsely ground
    pepper

⅔ cup extra virgin olive oil

Mix red wine vinegar, garlic, shallots, salt, oregano, basil and ground pepper in a food processor or blender until well blended. With processor running, add oil in a slow, steady stream and process until blended.

Preheat oven to 400°. Mix cheese and rosemary. Place 1 tablespoon cheese mixture on lightly greased baking sheet; spread slightly to flatten. Repeat with remaining cheese mixture. Allow 1 inch between each flattened crisp. Bake 5 minutes. Turn crisps over; bake an additional 1 minute or until golden brown. Cool on wire rack.

Place 1 cup greens on each plate. Top with 2 tablespoons grape halves and 2 tablespoons walnuts. Drizzle with 2 tablespoons dressing. Serve each salad with 2 crisps.

There's no doubt that when we talk about keeping your feet right underneath you, we are again contradicting some golf instructors. Many will instruct their students to take their stance wide. While this will make them very stable, they give up too much mobility to perform their best swing.

In our opinion, the majority of golf stances you see are too wide. In general as we age we loose flexibility. Needing all of the mobility we can get, too wide of a stance will inhibit our ability to move completely through the golf swing.

The next time you watch any sport, look at the athlete's foot position. In almost every case, just before they spring into action, they will get their feet right underneath them. This mobile stance allows for the most power and consistency in your swing.

Baby Greens with Avocado & Pears

2 oranges
3 tablespoons extra virgin olive oil
¾ teaspoon salt (optional)
¼ teaspoon coarsely ground
   black pepper

12 oz mixed baby greens
3 firm, ripe, pears, cored and cut
   into ½ inch pieces
2 ripe medium avocados, peeled
   and cut into ½ inch pieces

Cut the oranges in half and squeeze ½ cup juice into a large salad bowl. Grate the remaining peel to add 2 teaspoons of the zest to the orange juice. Add the oil, salt & pepper to the juice and whisk together.

Add the greens, pears and avocado. Toss together and serve immediately.

If you're ever lucky enough to find a certified osteopath who is also certified from the Institute of Physical Art, it's you lucky day. These well trained professionals are masters in functional manual therapy. Their technique to release and mobilize joints, reeducate the neuromuscular system, and just get you moving better is second to none. Unlike traditional physical therapists, they focus on the body as a whole rather than isolating a single problem. If you're struggling to improve on your own and want to become more functional, look one up today at www.ipaconed.com.

IT BAND STRETCH

Lie on your back with both feet hip width apart on the floor. Your arms should be straight out to the sides with your palms up. Cross your left leg all the way over your right leg. Then, roll your lower body to the right side as you look to you left. Rest in this position for one minute, and with every exhale, try to relax your back, hips and shoulders to give a little more into the stretch. Repeat on the other side. The perfect end postion of this stretch is when your left lower leg is on the floor, and your left arm and shoulder are on the floor. Keep relaxing as you get closer to this end. If you have two minutes for each side, that's great.

Winter Squash Soup

2 pounds winter squash, halved
  and seeded
2 onions, peeled and halved
1 bulb garlic, top cut off
1 teaspoon extra virgin olive oil
2 teaspoons dry or fresh thyme
Salt and pepper to taste

4 cups organic, fat free chicken
  broth
½ cup organic, low-fat plain
  yogurt (optional)
2 tablespoons chopped chives
  (optional)

Preheat the oven to 350°. Place squash, skin side down, in a glass baking dish, adding a little water to the bottom of the dish. Add onions and garlic, separated into cloves. Drizzle the garlic with olive oil and sprinkle the squash with thyme.

Cover dish with foil and put back into the oven for 1- 1½ hours, or until all of the vegetables are soft when pierced with a fork. Scoop the cooked squash out of the skin and place in a blender with the cooked onion and garlic, then puree until smooth.

Meanwhile, warm chicken broth in a large saucepan on the stove. Slowly stir in the pureed vegetables, and salt and pepper to taste. Serve hot with optional dollop of yogurt and chives. Serves 4.

Here's one more instance where many teaching professionals will disagree with us... SQUARE UP YOUR FEET! Often instructors will tell their students to point their left toe out, and we will disagree with them almost every time! Everting your left foot will change the position of your hips, cause stress on your knee, reduce your upper body rotation and inhibit your ability to transfer your weight effectively.

In a <u>functional</u> body, your feet should basically point forward (give or take 5 degrees). Having our feet pointed inward or outward invariably creates stress in our knees and hips, resulting in pain and compensating movements that result in a decrease in mobility and function. If squaring up your feet simply does not work for you, your hips are probably very tight. Take what your body will give, and evert your foot for now, but keep doing your Par For Life exercise recipe to gain more mobility throughout your hips and back, so you can increase the life span of your golf game.

Easy Chicken Noodle Soup

2 cups cubed cooked chicken or turkey

1 cup uncooked yolk-free whole wheat extra wide noodles

2 stalks celery, sliced

2 medium carrots, sliced

32 ounces organic low sodium chicken broth

Black pepper to taste

In a large saucepan bring chicken broth, black pepper, carrots and celery to a boil. Stir in noodles and chicken. Cook over medium heat for 10 minutes or until noodles are done.

Why train for golf when it's just a recreational pursuit? So that you can play as much as you want for as long as you like. Many non-golfers think the game is not at all demanding, just a walk in the park while you hit a little ball a couple of times. Golfers know better, and while it's not an aerobic exercise when you take a cart, a round of golf can leave you sore the next day.

The exercises from the Par For Life Institute are designed to keep your body functional, limber and strong, so that the strain your muscles endure during a round won't keep you off of the course the next day!

CATS & DOGS

After two stretches where we twist the spine from side to side, we always want to follow up with fluid front to back movement. Get on your hands and knees and make sure that your knees are directly under your hips and your hands directly under your shoulders. Inhale as you look up, collapsing your shoulders and low back closer to the ground - the Dog position. Exhale as you look down and stretch your entire back up in an arch - the Cat position. Repeat these in a fluid movement from one position to the other. Take care to make the stretch from your hip joint through your shoulders, neck and head engaging your entire spine.

French Onion Soup

¼ cup trans fat free margarine

3 medium onions, thinly sliced
(about 8 cups)

¼ teaspoon Stevia or
½ teaspoon Splenda®

2 tablespoons whole-wheat flour

2 cans beef consommé

5 cups organic beef broth

½ teaspoon powdered sage

1 bay leaf

½ cup dry red wine

8 half-inch thick slices of whole
wheat French bread

2 cups fresh grated provolone or
parmesan cheese

In a large saucepan, melt the margarine over medium heat. Stir in onions, cover and cook until translucent, about 10 minutes. Blend in Stevia or Splenda®. Cook over medium heat, stirring frequently until golden brown, about 25 minutes.

Sprinkle in the flour, stirring for another 3 minutes. Add broth, consommé, sage, bay leaf and red wine. Lower heat and simmer, uncovered, for another 30 minutes. Preheat the broiler while the soup is in its final simmer.

Ladle the soup into 4 oven-proof soup bowls. Arrange toast on top of soup and sprinkle generously with grated cheese. Place bowls on a cookie sheet and place under broiler until cheese is melted and golden brown. Serve immediately.

Now lets put all of the elements of a proper address position together:

1 - Grip your club, check your knuckle alignment and make sure your can move your wrist like a hinge.

2 - Get your toes pointed forward with your feet no more than shoulder width apart.

3 - Flex your knees slightly - keep them unlocked and ready for action.

4 - With a nice, natural s-curve in your back, tilt forward from your hips maintaining that curve.

5 - Check your weight on your feet - you want to make sure your weight is even front to back and left to right.

GREAT! Now you are stable, mobile, balanced and ready to transfer your weight, generate power, and knock that little white ball toward the hole!

Chicken Tortilla Soup

1 ½ pounds boneless, skinless chicken breasts

3 garlic cloves

1 large onion, chopped

1 green pepper, cored, seeded and chopped

2 celery stalks, finely chopped

1 jalapeno, minced

2 tablespoons extra light virgin olive oil

½ tablespoon ground coriander

2 cups organic blue corn chips

1 quart organic chicken broth

2 teaspoons Tabasco® sauce

½ cup non-fat plain yogurt

Juice and zest of 2 limes

4 scallions, white and green parts, thinly sliced

½ cup fresh cilantro leaves, chopped

Preheat a medium soup pot over medium-high heat and add olive oil. Chop chicken breasts into bite-size pieces. Season the chicken with salt and pepper if desired, and add to the hot soup pot. Lightly brown the chicken, about 3 to 4 minutes, add the garlic, green pepper, onions, jalapeno, celery, cumin, and coriander. Continue cooking for 3 minutes, stirring frequently.

While that is cooking, crush the tortilla chips in a sealable plastic bag. Add the ground tortilla chips to the soup pot and stir to combine. Add chicken stock and Tabasco® sauce and bring the soup to a simmer. Simmer the soup for about 15 minutes.

Garnish with yogurt, lime zest and juice, chopped cilantro and sliced scallions. Serves 4.

GRAVITY DROP

Stand on a stair or the back of your golf cart with the balls of your feet on the stair and your heels hanging off. Standing only on your toes and balancing yourself with your arms, drop your heels, feeling a stretch through the back of your leg. Make sure your ankles, hips, shoulder and ears are in a straight line perpendicular to the floor - often this may feel like you are leaning back.

As you hold this stretch for a minute and make sure that you are not leaning forward or back. Though the immediate stretch is felt in your calves, the benefits your body will reap is much greater. As you settle in this stretch, your joints will come back into alignment, reducing rotation as your hips settle in a very functional position.

Easy Gazpacho

4 Roma tomatoes, seeded, diced

1 each red and green bell peppers, cored, seeded and diced

1 cucumber, halved, seeded (not peeled) and chopped

4 green onions, green part only, thinly sliced

1 stalk of celery, chopped

½ red onion, finely chopped

4 garlic cloves, minced

1 jalapeno, cored, seeded and diced

6 cups (46 ounces) organic, low sodium tomato juice

½ cup white wine vinegar

1 ½ teaspoons freshly ground black pepper

½ teaspoons Tabasco® sauce

½ cup cilantro

Combine tomatoes, peppers, cucumbers, onions, celery, garlic and jalapeno in a large mixing bowl. If you prefer a spicier soup, leave the seeds in the jalapeno.

Stir in tomato juice, vinegar, black pepper and Tabasco®. Stir; chill at least 4 hours. The longer gazpacho sits, the more the flavors develop. Serve in bowls, garnish with cilantro. Serves 8

Now that you know how to address the ball, we're ready to talk about where the ball should be placed in your stance. We have found that traditional golf instruction seems to make this discussion far too complicated, virtually paralyzing the average golfer.

At the Par For Life Institute, we are all about function and movement, and paralysis has no place in our lives! Generally speaking, ball position is fairly simple. When hitting irons on a flat lie, keep the ball directly in the center of your stance (assuming that your stance is balanced and the center is in line with your spine). This allows you to catch the ball on a slightly descending blow.

From a tee, move the ball up a couple of inches (toward your forward foot). This allows for the club to catch the ball off of the tee with a slightly ascending blow. Unless you are trying to "create" a shot or impose a curve, stick to these simple fundamentals.

Many instructors will tell you to widen your stance to gain stability, but what you loose in mobility in this position will greatly limit the power you can create through the swing. The Par For Life Institute strongly advocates keeping your joints as close to their natural design as possible through your swing: shoulders over hips over knees over ankles.

To illustrate our point, we want to look at other athletes in motion. Non-golfers may laugh at the comparison of golfers to athletes, but it's a fact - you are one. The American Heritage Dictionary of the English Language defines an athlete as "a person possessing the natural or acquired traits, such as strength, agility and endurance, that are necessary for physical exercise or sport." If you're a golfer, you're an athlete. If you run on the treadmill, you're an athlete. Even if you will never win a contest or have an shred of hope of making the Olympics, you can still be an athlete. The game of golf is a sport, and the rules of sport need to apply to it.

 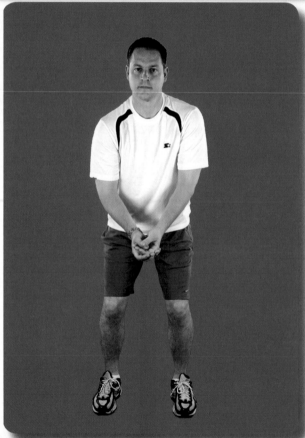 

Back to other athletic pursuits: Look at a basketball player, they may have a wide stance as they move side to side, but to make a shot, they get their feet right underneath them.

A volleyball player stays wide for the gentle sets, but for any power moves, you know where their feet are!

A tennis player does the same. A wide stance is maintained in the "ready" position, but the feet are right underneath them for the shot.

In short, in golf and any sport, a wide stance makes you LESS FUNCTIONAL and unable to perform to the best of your ability. If you've been wide for many years, it may feel odd at first to get your feet right under you, but it will pay off!

Remember that the key to having the proper ball position is to not complicate the issue. Simply put, with your irons, make sure the ball is placed right in the center of your stance. If you're on the tee, put the ball just a couple of inches forward of the center line, which will provide for a proper trajectory and more distance off of the tee.

As you advance in your game, there are other variations of your ball position which will allow you to create a fade or a draw, or address the dilemma of an uphill or downhill lie. For most shots, however, stick to these two simple principles and you'll set yourself up well for your game.

Playing your ball slightly behind the center of your stance may help you hit a lower trajectory golf shot. However, if not practiced and perfected, it is more likely to result in casting the club and hitting the ground behind the ball. It may also result in a reverse weight shift through your backswing, making a proper impact, release and finish difficult.

Placing the ball in the middle of your stance allows you to hit the ball with a slightly descending blow, creating the most consistent hit.

To maximize the distance off of a tee, you want to hit the ball not at the bottom of your swing arc, rather slightly on your upswing. This is why we place the tee a couple of inches forward of the center of your stance.

When using a tee, having the ball too far back in your stance produces similar results as you would see with your irons. Placing the ball too far forward produces inconsistent results, beginning with your address position being rotated to the left.

Practice Green
Geneva National Golf Club, Lake Geneva, Wisconsin

Main Courses & Full Swing

The main course makes the meal, and everything else is planned around it. So does the success of your full swing. Those long drives off of the tee that feel so good and can make or break the rest of your game.

As we plan our main courses, we focus on lean, high quality proteins like salmon and other fish, organic or free range chicken, turkey and lean beef. We like to find interesting recipes with great flavors, then adjust the fat and salt without compromising on the taste and texture.

When you are looking for meats, look for fresh, free range, and possibly organic cuts. Organically raised animals are given feed with none of the hormones and steroids that non-organic livestock are given. Antibiotics are given to organically raised animals only when needed, where in the average American farm, antibiotics are a part of the hormone, corn & oat mix. Avoid any "farm raised" fish, as they can as likely be injected with as many hormones and antibiotics as our farm-raised land animals.

If you have never before bought free range or organic meat, there are three things we need to prepare your for. One, it will be more expensive than regular meats as the organic or free range farms typically do not engage in mass production, and it costs more to feed an animal the natural food it needs rather than the inexpensive and drug laden feed. Two, the size may be an adjustment. An organically grown turkey, for instance, has not been raised with any of the breast meat enhancing hormones that are pumped into non-organic turkey, and as such may seem smaller. The third warning - organic meat, like organic fruits and vegetables, just tastes better.

For golf, we turn our focus to the full swing. Those great shots where you can give it all you've got and let the ball soar toward the hole. Remember your set-up and grip principles discussed earlier as the three will all work together to allow you to make Par For Life.

Player #5
Geneva National Golf Club
Lake Geneva, Wisconsin

Baked Chicken with Garlic & Sun Dried Tomatoes

4 boneless, skinless chicken breast halves (4 ounces each)

20 cloves garlic, peeled (about 2 heads)

1 medium onion, sliced ¼-inch-thick and separated into rings

½ cup chopped sun-dried tomatoes (not packed in oil)

¼ cup dry white wine

½ cup organic, low-fat chicken broth

1 teaspoon dried oregano

¼ teaspoon ground black pepper

Rinse the chicken, and pat it dry with paper towels. Coat a large oven-proof skillet with nonstick cooking spray, and preheat over medium-high heat. Crush 2 of the garlic cloves, and place them in the skillet. Place the chicken in the skillet, and arrange the remaining garlic cloves around the chicken.

Cook the chicken for about 2 minutes on each side, or until the chicken and garlic cloves are nicely browned. Remove the chicken from the skillet, and set aside. Remove the skillet from the heat.

Lay the onions and tomatoes over the garlic cloves in the skillet. Arrange the chicken in a single layer over the tomatoes, onions, and garlic. Pour the wine and broth over the chicken, and sprinkle with the oregano and pepper.

Cover and bake at 350° for 30 minutes, or until the chicken is tender and the juices run clear when the chicken is pierced. Serve hot, accompanying each chicken breast with some of the vegetables and pan juices. Serve over brown rice or noodles if desired. Serves 4.

The series of exercises we give you in the Soup & Salad section is a very general one, designed for the functional golfer to get them warmed up to take on the range, or even the first tee.

We have seen from experience both with ourselves and hundreds of clients that you will feel great after this session, and you will hit the range warmed up like you've already hit a bucket of balls.

That being said, we also know that your results will be even better if you receive a routine specifically designed for you. When we mean you, we don't mean people like you or with the same body type as you... we mean YOU.

Through this section, we will explain what we look at for our individual clients, and how you can get a personal assessment from the experts at the Par For Life Institute.

Supplementation of garlic has shown to improve cholesterol levels, immune function, circulation, liver function, nervous system, enhanced growth of beneficial bacteria, and shown as a stress reducer. There are numerous brands and blends readily available, and our favorite choice is Kyloic, Formula 100. Remember, there is no one magic pill. The body works in synergy, take a balanced approach to food and supplementation.

Chicken with Black Bean Salsa

6 boneless, skinless chicken breast halves (4 ounces each)
1 tablespoon crushed fresh garlic
¼ teaspoon ground black pepper
3 tablespoons organic low-fat chicken broth
1 can (15 ounces) organic black beans, not drained
½ cup salsa or picante sauce
3 tablespoons thinly sliced scallions

Rinse the chicken and pat it dry with paper towels. Spread some garlic on each piece, and sprinkle with the pepper.

Coat a large skillet with nonstick cooking spray, and preheat over medium-high heat. Arrange the chicken in the skillet, and cook for about 2 minutes on each side, or until nicely browned. Reduce the heat to low, and add the broth. Cover and simmer for 10 to 12 minutes, or until the chicken is tender and the juices run clear when the chicken is pierced. Transfer the chicken to a serving platter, and cover to keep warm.

Drain any liquid from the skillet, and add the undrained black beans and the salsa or picante sauce. Cook and stir over medium heat until heated through. Spoon the bean mixture over the chicken, sprinkle with the scallions, and serve hot, accompanying the dish with brown rice if desired. Serves: 6

In nearly every sport, instructors will teach students to use their large muscle groups to produce power. Golf is no different. Being able to hit the ball far and straight is the golfer's first priority. To accomplish this, we need to be able to use our major muscle groups to transfer weight from our evenly balanced address position to the right (loading) and back to the left (unleashing the power), while the arms and hands hang on for the ride.

To understand and teach the body this basic weight transfer movement, we begin practicing without a club in our Cross-Arm Drill. For this drill, stand straight up with your feet hip to shoulder width apart. Cross your arms comfortably across your chest with your hands on your upper arms. This position will allow the golfer to feel a dynamic weight shift without worrying about their grip and club position. Transfer your weight from right to left and back again. If you are not sure if you are fully transferring your weight, transfer to your right side and pick up your left foot — can you without falling over? Try the same thing on your left side. Once you get the feel of the drill and are truly transferring your weight while standing straight up, slightly flex your knees and tilt your upper body forward as if you are addressing the ball, then continue the drill, transferring your weight from right to left and back again.

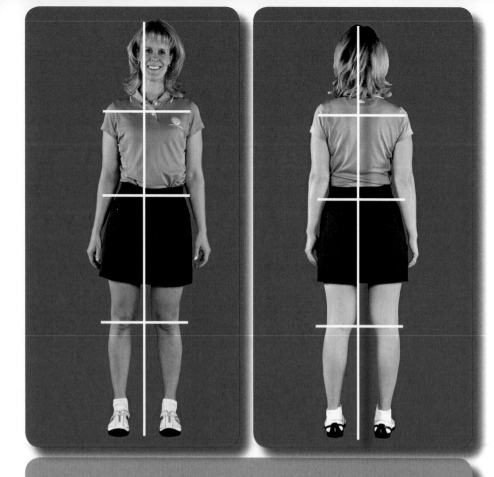

Salmon with Scalloped Sweet Potatoes

3 medium sweet potatoes, peeled and thinly sliced (about 4 cups)

1 medium yellow onion, roughly chopped

1 teaspoon grated ginger root

1 cup freshly squeezed orange juice

3 tablespoons orange marmalade, 1 tablespoon reserved

Salt to taste

2 tablespoons melted trans fat free margarine

1 ¼ pounds salmon fillet, skin removed, cut into 6 pieces

Freshly ground black pepper, to taste

¼ cup organic almond slivers, toasted

¼ cup Italian parsley sprigs

Preheat oven to 400°. Combine sweet potatoes, onion, ginger, juice, 2 tablespoons marmalade, margarine and salt. Place in a 9 X 13 inch casserole dish, coated with cooking spray. Bake, covered, for 40 minutes.

Remove casserole from the oven and place the salmon on top. Brush fish with remaining 1 tablespoon marmalade and grind on the black pepper. Return to oven uncovered and bake 10 to 12 minutes, until fish is done to your liking. Garnish with almonds and parsley.

When a client comes to the Par For Life Institute, we take a little different approach than the average golf instructor. We ask the basic questions... How long have you been a golfer? What are your misses like? What are your good shots like? What's your handicap? Etc. We talk about when & how you like to golf and what your goals of our instruction are. After that, we diverge from the norm.

We ask about your aches and pains. We ask if you get fatigued during your game or other activities. Next we ask you to stand against a wall and we look at you from the front, back and both sides. We even take pictures to get a better look and to measure progress.

From the front view we draw a line perpendicular to the ground up from the middle of the stance. This should bisect the body perfectly evenly. Straight lines drawn through both knees, both hips, both shoulders and both ears should all be parallel to the ground. Finally both kneecaps should point forward. More often than not, all of these criteria are not met.

Grilled Mahi Mahi with Cilantro Marinade

1 ½ pounds Mahi Mahi
1 bunch cilantro, chopped
Juice of one lemon

3 garlic cloves, minced
¼ cup extra virgin olive oil
¼ teaspoon black pepper

Mix the cilantro, lemon juice, cloves, olive oil and pepper together.

Brush both sides of Mahi Mahi with the marinade and let stand, covered, in refrigerator for several hours. Grill under broiler or on the grill for 5 to 10 minutes per side, depending on thickness of fish. Be careful not to let the fish burn. Serve with organic brown rice.

Be sure to maintain your upper body tilt at the top of your backswing in the drill and while golfing. Many, if not most, golfers find this abundantly difficult, and we see many of our students struggling with this position. Difficult or not, maintaining a properly balanced upper body tilt throughout the golf swing is necessary to a successful game. If you find it difficult to maintain a proper tilt throughout your swing, keep practicing in a mirror so you can see and feel the weight transfer. More importantly, you need to become more functional and strong through your low back and hips, so make sure to do your daily and pre-round Par For Life Exercise Recipe to get your body into prime golfing shape.

With all of the reports of polluted oceans and streams breeding contaminated and toxic fish, it can be hard to discern which types of fish are still good for you. When choosing your fresh fish, buy varieties from Alaska, Australia and New Zealand, whose waters have the lowest pollutants. Avoid farmed fish, and avoid swordfish, lake whitefish, oysters, mussels, clams, large tuna species, yellow fin and big-eye, as they tend to have higher mercury and contaminant levels. Skipjack, albacore, flounder and sole are four of the "cleanest" available species today.

When we look at clients from the side view, we draw a line from just in front of the ankle bone up perpendicularly from the ground. This line should cross directly through the knee, hip, shoulder and ear. Comparing the right and left sides, the lines should look the same. Again, more often than not, we see many deviations from the ideal posture.

Since the game of golf requires an extreme amount of bilateral function as we rotate through the golf swing, these deviations from right to left will no doubt make themselves known on the course.

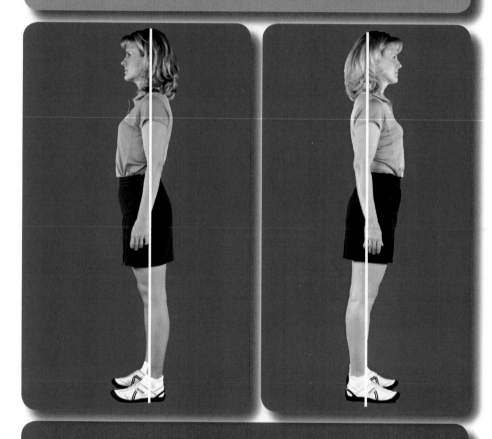

Inflammation – A leading cause of death? Books are written on it and scientists are now agreeing with it. It's time that YOU pay attention as well. Make sure you include a C-Reactive Protein blood test with your annual visit to the doctor, which measures the amount of chronic inflammation in your body. If your CRP reading is outside the optimal range, take charge of your health and make the necessary adjustments without delay. Foods rich in Omega-3 fatty acids, like salmon, work as inflamation reducers in your body. Its not as simple as taking extra ibuprofen, get the facts to ensure your longevity.

Marinated Grilled Salmon

1 one-pound fresh wild salmon fillet with the skin on	1 tablespoon extra virgin olive oil
¼ cup reduced sodium soy sauce	1 ½ tablespoons organic honey
⅓ cup rice vinegar	¼ cup red onion, finely diced
¼ cup water	½ teaspoon dill weed
	1 ½ tablespoons fresh lemon juice

Place the salmon, skin side up in a glass baking pan. In a small bowl combine the soy sauce, vinegar, water, oil, honey, and onion. Pour the mixture over the fish and marinate in the refrigerator for ½ to 1 hour. Baste the fish frequently.

Transfer the fish to a medium-high grill, skin side down, and discard the remaining marinade. Grill the fish for 10 minutes per inch, flipping it over halfway through.

Halibut with Sun-Dried Tomatoes & Olives

6 halibut steaks
Extra virgin olive oil for grilling
Salt and pepper
1 small red onion, peeled and
    chopped
4 cloves garlic, peeled and
    crushed

½ cup extra virgin olive oil
3 tablespoons balsamic vinegar
¼ cup oil packed sun-dried
    tomatoes, drained and
    coarsely chopped
1 cup black olives, pitted and
    coarsely chopped

Place a ½ cup of extra virgin olive oil in a small skillet over medium heat and add the onion. Cook, stirring occasionally, until the onion is soft. Add the garlic and cook for two more minutes. Remove the pan from the heat and pour the contents into a medium-sized serving bowl. Add the vinegar, tomatoes, and olives. Season with salt and pepper. Keep at room temperature while grilling the fish.

Brush one side of the fish with olive oil, then season with salt and pepper. Place the fish, oiled-side down on a hot grill and cook for about 4 minutes. Brush the top of the fish with more olive oil, then season it. Turn the fish and grill another few minutes until just cooked through. Serve with the tomato-olive mixture.

We use our second drill, the Cylinder Drill to teach the smooth and effective transfer your weight to your right leg in your back swing, through impact and ending with your weight on your left leg.

Hold a six-inch foam roll parallel to your torso. Flex your knees and tilt at your hips as if you are addressing the ball. Rotate your trunk and transfer your body weight to the right, as if you are turning into your backswing, using the foam roll as a guide to keep your body square. Next transfer your weight through and to the left, again using the roll as your guide. Repeat this drill, right to left and back again, to experience a proper weight transfer while truly maintaining your pelvic tilt. Being able to effectively transfer your weight and load on to your right side during your back swing is similar to a prize fighter putting his weight on the back foot as he gets ready to explode with a mighty blow. This is the first essential motion that creates power in your swing.

Halibut with Cilantro & Lime

1 pound halibut, tuna or
    swordfish steaks
2 tablespoons fresh lime juice
¼ cup Braggs Liquid Aminos or
    reduced sodium soy sauce
1 teaspoon cornstarch
½ teaspoon minced fresh ginger

1 tablespoon extra virgin olive oil
½ cup slivered red or yellow
    onion
2 cloves garlic, minced
¼ cup coarsely chopped fresh
    cilantro
Lime wedges optional

Cut halibut into 1-inch pieces and sprinkle with lime juice.

Place liquid aminos or soy sauce in a cup with the cornstarch and blend until smooth. Stir in ginger and set aside.

Heat oil in wok or large nonstick skillet over medium heat until hot. Add onion and garlic and stir-fry 2 minutes. Add the halibut and stir-fry for another 2 minutes or until fish flakes easily when tested with fork.

Stir soy sauce mixture again and add to wok. Stir-fry everything together for another 30 seconds or until sauce boils and thickens. Sprinkle with cilantro and garnish with the lime wedges if desired.

On the right side of this book, you will see how we look at posture in the golf stance, and how important it is to your swing. On this side, we will stick to general posture principles.

What we know is that holding a proper posture is more than just aesthetically pleasing. Maintaining a proper posture allows your body to achieve maximum function with minimum stress on your joints. What we have all come to believe are normal aches and pains of aging are more often then not a result of our joints being out of alignment which causes stress on the associated muscles and joints.

Is a calorie a calorie? In our opinion, no. The "bomb calorimeter" measures the heat given off when an item is burned, and it is what we use to determine the number of calories in our food. Rather than anything resembling the human body, we base all of our standard labeling practice on a super hot oven. The claim is 9 calories for a gram of fat and 4 calories per gram of a carbohydrate or protein. Have you ever known someone who just looks at a brownie and gains weight, or the thin person who eats like a horse and never seems to gain an ounce?

Bottom line, the human body is not a calorimeter, and your personal metabolism plus the make-up of your diet, your hormonal health, and even your mitochondrial health will determine how much you can burn in a day. Counting calories is out, eating quality food is in.

Seared Tuna with Citrus Relish

4 4-ounce fresh tuna steaks,
  ¾ inch thick
Sea salt (optional)
Black pepper (optional)
2 teaspoons organic white wine
  vinegar
2 teaspoons reduced sodium soy
  sauce
½ teaspoon fresh ginger, grated

1 tablespoon extra virgin olive oil
1 medium red grapefruit, peeled
  and sliced
1 medium orange, peeled and
  sliced
2 tablespoons red onion, finely
  chopped
2 tablespoons cilantro, chopped
2 teaspoons extra virgin olive oil

Rinse fish; pat dry with paper towels. If desired, season fish with salt and pepper. Set aside.

For citrus relish, in a small bowl, combine vinegar, soy sauce, and ginger. Whisk in 1 tablespoon olive oil. Cut grapefruit sections into fourths and coarsely chop orange slices. Stir fruit, red onion, and cilantro into vinegar mixture. Set aside.

In a large skillet heat the 2 teaspoons olive oil over medium-high heat. Add fish and cook for 3 to 4 minutes on each side or until fish flakes easily or until desired doneness. Serve fish with citrus relish. Serves 4.

By now you've learned how to transfer or load your weight to the right for a functional and powerful backswing. As you start your backswing, focus on the proper weight transfer and allow the club to take its natural path.

What's your key thought for you as you start your backswing? Some golfers believe the backswing begins with the left shoulder pushing away. Others feel the left knee moving toward the right is the start of the swing. Still others say it begins with a slight movement of the head to the right. Depending on a golfer's function, the first move of their backswing will vary. After looking at hours of video and thousands of still shots, we believe that the best, most powerful golfers immediately load their weight on to their right side, allowing them to effectively transfer their weight through the swing and fly the ball down the fairway.

With all of that to think about, take care not to paralyze your self with thoughts. Learn and practice a smooth, consistent weight transfer back to your right and through to your left - that's enough.

BBQ Chicken Pizza

1 pound boneless, skinless chicken breasts, cubed

1 tablespoon extra virgin olive oil

¼ cup plus 2 tablespoons favorite BBQ sauce

1 cup shredded mozzarella cheese

1 tablespoon fresh grated parmesan cheese

¼ cup red onion, thinly sliced

2 tablespoons cilantro, chopped

1 clove garlic, minced

1 large whole wheat thin crust pizza shell (such as Boboli)

To prepare the chicken using a large skillet, heat the olive oil on medium to high heat. Add chicken and sauté until cooked, about 5-6 minutes. Set aside in refrigerator and until chilled through. Coat chicken with 2 tablespoons barbecue sauce. Set aside.

Preheat the oven to 425°. Spread ¼ cup barbecue sauce over the surface of the pizza crust. Distribute parmesan cheese and ¾ cup of mozzarella cheese over the sauce. Distribute most of the chicken over the cheese. Place onions and garlic over the chicken pieces. Sprinkle remainder ¼ cup of the mozzarella cheese.

Transfer pizza to the oven, bake until crust is crisp and golden and the cheese at the center is bubbly, 8 to 10 minutes. When the pizza is cooked, carefully remove it from the oven; sprinkle with cilantro over the hot surface. Slice and serve.

Since misalignments in our joints are responsible for so many aches and pains, and those aches and pains are responsible for our gradual decrease in activities as we age, a goal of the Par For Life Institute is to create better joint alignments, decreasing overall discomforts and adding to our golf longevity. Our mission is to give you the tools to be able to golf as much as you want for as long as you like, and the instruction on how to improve the position of your joint is one of our greatest tools.

Before we are able to help improve the positions of your joints, we first need to aliviate any persistent pain present. As many of us, unfortunately, know by experience, back pain can be absolutely debilitating, and no progress can be made if your back kills you at the end of your day or your round. So, before we progress on to how we address and improve the posture of individual clients, we need to give you a few tools to decrease immediate pain.

The exercises on the following pages serve two purposes. One, if you are presently experiencing back pain, get into one of these positions and you should feel relief. Secondly, and probably more importantly, these four basic positions serve to get your hips and shoulders into a more proper alignment not only for the moment, but throughout the day and into the next.

The Perfect Swing – There's no such destination, but the journey sure is fun. The fact is that you can grip the club with a long left thumb, loop the club from the inside into a perfect downswing, have a reverse pivot, setup with a wide or narrow stance, swing the handle, swing on plane, setup with the weight on the heels, etc, etc, etc. The point is that there any many ways of hitting the golf ball and playing good golf. What we see at the Par for Life Institute is that your swing (pattern of movement) is based on your function or dysfunction of your body. Become more functional, and you will become more consistent!

Apple & Pork Skewers

1 pound pork tenderloin
2 red or golden delicious apples
1 lemon
1 tablespoon fresh squeezed
   lemon juice
2 teaspoons whole grain mustard
2 teaspoons Dijon mustard

2 tablespoons apple cider vinegar
2 tablespoons extra virgin olive oil
2 tablespoons whole grain
   mustard
2 tablespoons Dijon mustard
6 tablespoons nonfat plain yogurt

Combine 2 tablespoons of the whole grain mustard and 2 tablespoons of the Dijon mustard. Slowly add the yogurt and blend until well mixed. Let stand or chill until needed.

Cut the tenderloin into bite sized pieces. Core the apples & cut into thick wedges. Toss the apples with the extra lemon juice. Cut the lemon into very thin slices.

Wrap a piece of pork in a lemon slice, resembling a taco, and thread onto a metal skewer. Alternate apples and pork-lemon pieces to fill four skewers.

Mix the remaining mustards, vinegar and olive oil together well. Brush onto each skewer.

Grill the skewers on a hot grill, or under a preheated broiler, for 10-15 minutes until the meat is cooked through. Continue brushing the skewers with the marinade throughout the cooking time.

Place the skewers on warm plates and drizzle with the mustard yogurt sauce. Serves 4

Do you know your Hemoglobin level? Make sure to ask your doctor to look at Hemoglobin A1C in your annual blood testing. It measures the past two or three months of glucose status, identifying risk of heart disease whether you have diabetes or not.

Many golfers have a tendency to tense up the moment the club is placed into their hands. Remember, golf works best with a light grip pressure and a relaxed body, truly allowing for the coil and release of the swing. Tour players reduce the tension by a variety of methods, mostly by "waggling" their club or keeping their feet moving before starting their backswing. This is no different than the tennis player bouncing between hits to be ready for the next. Never start from a static position – always keep your body in a dynamic position.

Ginger Soy Strip Steaks

½ cup reduced sodium soy
   sauce

3 garlic cloves, minced

1 teaspoon black pepper

2 tablespoons lemon juice

1 tablespoon minced fresh ginger

4 beef strip steaks,
   each 1-inch thick

Stir together the first five ingredients in a shallow dish. Add the steaks, turning to coat completely with the marinade. Cover and chill for 30 minutes on each side.

Remove the steaks from the marinade, and discard any remaining liquid. Grill, with the lid closed, over medium-high heat 4 minutes on each side or to the desired temperature. Serves 4

High cholesterol is certainly a concern for many people. Listening to pharmaceutical commercials and the news, however, you would think that cholesterol is the only indicator you should look at to predict heart disease. This is simply not the case, and two tests your doctor should include in your annual blood test may even be better predictors of heart problems than the popular cholesterol test. C-Reactive Protein measures chronic inflammation in the body, and is one major predictors of cardio-vascular disease. Homocysteine levels are mainly associated with an increased risk of heart attack. Get these two in line, along with keeping your cholesterol in check, and you should have healthy heart for years.

BACK SETTLE

The Back Settle position is the simplest position to get into when you are experiencing pain, using the floor to relax your back and realign your hips and shoulders in a completely passive position. Lie on your back and place both of your lower legs on a chair, ottoman or couch. Your legs should be bent at 90° angles at both the hips and knees. Keep your feet hip width apart and pointed up as you allow your back to relax into the position. You may find that your lower back is arched off of the ground at the beginning and flattens after a few minutes. For a healthy back, get into the back settle position for five minutes every day, and up to thirty minutes for pain relief.

Grilled Salmon Kebobs with Dill

2 10-ounce center cut wild
    salmon fillets, skinned
12 cherry tomatoes
2 medium zucchinis, cut into ¾
    inch rounds

8 tablespoons extra virgin olive oil
1/3 cup dry white wine
2 teaspoons garlic, minced
2 tablespoons fresh dill, chopped
Salt and pepper

Lightly oil the grill and preheat. Pat salmon dry and cut into cubes. In a large shallow bowl, whisk together the ingredients for the marinade. Add the salmon, tomatoes and zucchini and toss well to coat evenly. Cover and let stand at room temperature for 20 minutes. Alternately thread salmon, zucchini and tomatoes onto skewers. Grill the kebobs on an oiled rack turning to cook until salmon is cooked through, about six to eight minutes. This recipe can also be done in the oven and broiled.

Once you reach the top of your backswing, the power begins. The downswing is initiated by the transfer of weight from your right side to your left. The move that begins the downswing is debatable, some say it starts at the foot, some say the hips begin the move, and still others believe it's the upper body. Focusing on the minute detail that starts the downswing is almost folly. What you need to concentrate on is rotating your torso to the left and allowing your weight to fully transfer with the rotation. This turn in your upper and lower body and full weight transfer to the left helps to maintain the delay or power through your downswing and on to impact.

Healthy Chicken Enchiladas

1 cooked rotisserie chicken	1 tomato, diced
24 ounces reduced fat Mexican blend shredded cheese	2 tablespoons whole wheat flour
1 large can of low sodium enchilada sauce	2 tablespoons trans fat free margarine
12 whole wheat flour tortillas	1 cup water
	Extra virgin olive oil

When the cooked chicken is cool enough to touch, remove meat from the bones (that's the messy part). Place chicken in a skillet, add margarine and brown the chicken. Add water and fresh diced tomatoes. Simmer until the chicken becomes stringy and all the moisture has been absorbed.

In a separate pan, heat up the enchilada sauce and add a little flour to help thicken. After sauce has thickened, remove from heat and allow to cool. When both the sauce and chicken has cooled, start quick frying your tortillas in a small bit of oil, not allowing the tortillas to get hard.

In a separate bowl, place 5 tablespoons of sauce in a 13x9x2 inch baking dish enough to cover the bottom. Brush both sides of each tortilla with extra sauce and fill with 2 tablespoons chicken mixture and 2-3 tablespoons of cheese. Roll and place if baking dish. When dish is full, spread a little sauce over enchiladas and sprinkle with remainder of cheese.

Bake at 350° for 20 to 30 minutes until cheese has melted. Garnish with extra sauce, green onion, black olives and non-fat plain yogurt.

SUPINE GROIN STRETCH
The Supine Groin Stretch takes a little longer than the back settle because we stretch both sides independently. Lie on your back with only one leg up on the chair or ottoman. This leg should be bent at 90° angles at both the hip and knee. Your other leg should be straight out on the floor. Throughout the stretch, keep both legs straight out from the hip joint with your toes pointed upwards. Relax your arms out at about a 45° angle from your shoulders with your palms up. This allows your shoulders to fully relax into the ground. Relax in this position for at least 5 minutes on each side, and up to 15 minutes per side for the greatest benefits.

A ready to eat avocado is slightly soft but should have no dark sunken spots or cracks. A firm, less mature fruit can be ripened at home and may be less likely to have bruises when it is ready to be eaten. Ripen in a paper bag at room temperature for a couple of days. As the fruit ripens, the skin may turn darker. Avocados should not be refrigerated until they are ripe. Once ripe, they can be kept refrigerated for up to a week if they have not been sliced.
    Add plenty of avocado to your diet in salads, dips and dressings, and enjoy the benefits of this tasty fruit.

Pan Seared Scallops with Lemon Vinaigrette

12 ounces fresh sea scallops

1 lemon

1 pound fresh asparagus spears, cut into 2-inch pieces

1 medium red onion, sliced into thin wedges

3 tablespoons extra virgin olive oil

2 or 3 fresh basil sprigs

Salt and pepper to taste

Rinse scallops, pat dry with paper towels and set aside.

Remove peel from lemon and scrape off white portion. Cut peel into very thin strips and set aside. Squeeze 2 tablespoons juice from the lemon and set the juice aside.

In a large skillet cook the asparagus and red onion in 1 tablespoon of the olive oil for 2 to 3 minutes or until tender, but still a little crisp. Season to taste with salt and pepper. Transfer the asparagus mixture to a serving platter and keep warm.

In the same skillet combine reserved lemon peel, the remaining 2 tablespoons olive oil, and the basil sprigs. Cook until heated through, about 1 minute. Remove and discard the lemon peel and basil sprigs with a slotted spoon, reserving the olive oil.

Cook the scallops in the hot, flavored olive oil for 3 to 5 minutes or until scallops are opaque, turning once. Stir in reserved lemon juice and asparagus mixture and serve. Serves 4

As you start rotating and loading to the left, we see the golfer's moment of truth - Impact! Your weight transferring to the left adds power and mass to the impact. From the front view, notice how the weight has moved left. From the side view, the position of the body at impact shows the hips are left, or open to the target line, and the shoulders are aimed down the target line or slightly left. As a general observation, we see shorter golfers tend to have their bodies more open to the target line at impact than taller golfers.

Honey-Lime Glazed Salmon with Bean & Corn Salad

1 medium red onion, chopped
2 garlic cloves, chopped
½ teaspoon red pepper flakes
1 teaspoon ground cumin
4 tablespoons extra virgin olive oil
Juice of 2 limes
Salt and pepper
3 tablespoons organic honey
1 teaspoon chili powder
4 6-ounce wild salmon fillets
1 red bell pepper, cored, seeded, and chopped
1 10 oz bag frozen corn kernels, defrosted
½ cup organic low-fat chicken broth
1 15-ounce can organic black beans, rinsed and drained
3 tablespoons fresh cilantro leaves, chopped
6 cups baby spinach

In a preheated medium skillet over medium heat add 2 tablespoons olive oil. Add the onions, garlic, red pepper flakes, cumin, salt, and pepper. Cook, stirring occasionally, for 3 minutes.

In a second preheated medium skillet over medium-high heat, add remaining 2 tablespoons olive oil. In a shallow dish, combine the juice of one lime, honey, chili powder, salt and pepper. Add the salmon fillets to the lime-honey mixture and toss to coat thoroughly. Place the salmon in the hot skillet and heat until cooked through, about 4 minutes on each side.

To the cooked onions, add the bell peppers and corn kernels and cook for 1 minute. Add the chicken broth and continue to cook for an additional 2 minutes. Add the black beans and cook until heated through. Remove the skillet from the heat and add the remaining juice from the second lime, the cilantro, and spinach. Toss to wilt the spinach. Serve the glazed salmon on top of the black bean and corn salad.

The Back Settle and Supine Groin positions as described in the previous pages are best for people with an anterior or neutral pelvic tilt. For those of you with a posterior pelvic tilt, our Need Greens in Regulation golfers, we like to add a small roll under the lumbar spine to remind the body of the natural s-curve that may be missing. People with a posterior tilt tend to have a "flat" back instead of the natural, functional curves, and we want to restore the body's natural position. If you are among this group, roll a hand towel into about a 3-inch roll and place it under your lumbar spine as you relax into the Back Settle or Supine Groin positions as described earlier.

Pan Grilled Salmon Cakes

1 pound cooked wild salmon fillets, flaked, boned and skinless

¾ cup seasoned dried bread crumbs

½ cup minced scallions (white part and 2" of green)

1 teaspoon grated fresh ginger

3 egg whites or egg substitute equivalent

2 teaspoons Dijon mustard

¼ teaspoon black pepper

2 teaspoons extra virgin olive oil

In a mixing bowl, combine the salmon, bread crumbs, scallions, ginger, egg whites, mustard, and pepper, and mix well. Form into 4 cakes.

In a large nonstick skillet, heat the oil over medium-high heat. Reduce the heat to medium, and sauté the cakes for about 4 minutes on each side. Serves 4

Before we continue, we want to take a moment to review our proper set-up position. Get your grip right, and address the ball by slightly breaking your knees and tilting from the hips, bringing your upper body down toward the ball. In your tilt, your back should display the natural "s" curve of your spine.

Everyone knows that fish is a great source of lean protein and good fats not normally found in other meats. We hear, however, people who have hesitations to prepare fish at home because they don't know how to buy it. Here's some tips to make it easier. First and foremost, fish should not smell "fishy." That said, only buy fish from a better market where it is on ice, not pre-packaged so you can do a sniff test for yourself. Look to make sure the fish is on the ice, not piled well off of the ice, and that cooked and raw fish are displayed separately. Finally, if you buy a whole fish, make sure it still looks "healthy," with great color and bright, full eyes. Make fish part of your regular at home menu and reap the health benefits.

Apple Cider Chicken

4 6-ounce boneless, skinless free-range chicken breast halves

3 tablespoons extra virgin olive oil

2 medium yellow onions, thinly sliced

2 tablespoons fresh thyme leaves, chopped

3 tablespoons organic honey

3 large garlic cloves, chopped

½ cup apple cider vinegar

2 cups organic low fat chicken broth

Black pepper

Preheat a large skillet over medium-high heat. Add 2 tablespoons of olive oil. Season chicken with pepper and add to the hot skillet. Brown the chicken on both sides, about 3 minutes per side. Remove the meat from the pan, and cover to keep warm.

Add one tablespoon of olive oil, onions, thyme, honey, and garlic to the hot pan. Season the onions with salt and pepper and cook, stirring frequently for 7 to 8 minutes. The onions should get brown and caramelized. Add the cider vinegar and the chicken broth. Turn up the heat to high and bring the liquids up to a simmer. Return the chicken to the skillet and cook in the sauce for about 10 minutes, flipping the chicken over halfway through the cooking time.

Arrange chicken breasts on serving plates. Pour generous amounts of sauce with the onions over the chicken.

WALL SIT

The Wall Sit is a more demanding exercise, but is also an easier position to achieve if you are not able to lay down. If your lower back aches on the golf course, you can even do a quick Wall Sit against your golf cart mid-round. Place your back against a wall and slide down until you have a 90° angle at your hips and knees, as if you are sitting on a chair. Flatten your low back into the wall and hold this position for one minute or more.

If you frequently experience low back or hip pain while you are walking, the Wall Sit is a great move to do anywhere. We may look a little silly, but you can spot our clients out in public, taking a quick one minute seat on the wall. It resets the hips into a more functional position, reduces rotation and takes the weight off of the lower back for a moment. Try it, and be prepared for someone to look at you funny while they offer you a chair.

Sirloin Strips with Portabello Mushrooms

12 ounces free range
   top sirloin steaks
12 ounces portabello
   mushrooms, sliced
½ cup burgundy or other
   dry red wine
3 tablespoons low sodium soy
   sauce

3 tablespoons Worcestershire
   sauce
6 medium garlic cloves, minced
2 teaspoons extra virgin olive oil
½ tablespoon dried oregano

To prepare the steaks, discard all visible fat and cut into thin strips. Combine the marinade ingredients in a large resealable plastic bag. Add the mushrooms and beef to the marinade. Seal and turn to coat. Refrigerate for 30 minutes, turning the bag frequently.

Meanwhile, heat a large skillet over medium high heat for about 1 minute. Transfer beef mixture to the skillet. Cook for 4 minutes, or until the meat is no longer pink, stirring frequently. Return heat to high and cook for 5 minutes, stirring occasionally. Remove from heat. Serve with spinach fettuccine or your favorite whole wheat pasta. Serves 4

Impact is a direct result of your grip, address position and weight transfer. If any one of these three is less than ideal, the club position at the moment of impact will be effected. Through the downswing, notice that the weight is moving left and the hands are slightly ahead of the ball at impact due to the powerful rotation of the body. The hips are rotating left of the target line, and all of this is done while the upper body has maintained the proper pelvic tilt.

Injuries can stop you cold. You can't practice, play or train when injured, and the effects can last for some time. If you do get injured, remember RICE for improvement. RICE stands for Rest, Ice, Compression, and Elevation. After feeling better get to a Par for Life professional for a recipe of therapy.

Citrus Roasted Salmon

¼ cup fresh squeezed organic orange juice

¼ cup dry white wine or sherry

2 tablespoons fresh tarragon (or 1 teaspoon dried)

1 tablespoon trans fat free margarine, softened

1 clove garlic, minced

4 large boneless salmon fillets, skin removed

Salt and pepper to taste

Stir orange juice, sherry or wine, tarragon, margarine, salt, pepper, and garlic until well combined. Do not use cooking wine or sherry, the sodium content is too high. Brush all over the fish. Cover and let stand in the refrigerator for 1 to 4 hours.

Preheat oven to 425°. Place the fish on an oiled baking sheet and brush evenly with the orange mixture in the marinating pan. Place on center rack of the oven and cook for 8 to 10 minutes or until the fish flakes easily and is coral colored in the center. Perfect with steamed asparagus and brown rice.

THE MARATHON

The psosas muscle is probably the single most important muscle related to posture, and it is, unfortunately, a difficult muscle to stretch because of its location. This muscle basically attaches your upper and lower bodies together, going roughly from your spine, through your pelvis to your femur.

A too tight or too strong psosas often results in a anterior pelvic tilt, and an over stretched or weak psosas give us the posterior pelvic tilt. Because of its importance, if you could only do one stretch a day, the Marathon would be the one we choose for you. The trick is that it's a long one (one-half hour) and it requires a step stool and a chair. Though its time consuming, its well worth it.

Lie on your back with one leg straight on the ground and your other foot resting on the top level of the stair. Keep both legs hip width apart with your toes pointed upward. Relax here for five minutes, then lower your leg to the next level. Repeat on every level, including the floor, then switch legs. Toward the end of each five minutes, you should feel your lower back relaxing into the floor.

Grilled Chicken Parmigiana

2 pounds free range chicken breast cutlets

3 garlic cloves, chopped

1 teaspoon crushed red pepper flakes

1 small yellow onion, finely chopped

1 can (28 ounces) organic fire-roasted diced tomatoes

10 fresh basil leaves (about 1 cup), shredded

½ cup freshly grated parmesan cheese

½ pound smoked mozzarella, thinly sliced

2 tablespoons extra virgin olive oil for drizzling

Salt and pepper to taste

Heat an outdoor grill. Season the chicken with salt and pepper and drizzle a small amount of olive oil to keep it from sticking to the grill. Cook for 3 to 4 minutes on each side and transfer to a platter then cover with plastic wrap. While chicken is cooking, prepare the sauce.

Place a medium pot on the stove over medium heat with 2 tablespoons of olive oil. Add the garlic, red pepper flakes, and onion. Cook for 10 minutes, stirring often. Add the tomatoes and heat through, about 2 minutes. Wilt in the basil and season the sauce with salt and pepper if needed.

Preheat the broiler to high. Layer the chicken with the tomato sauce in a casserole dish. Top the chicken with parmesan and mozzarella. Brown the casserole under the broiler for 3 minutes.

Performing the golf swing requires a great deal of bilateral function in the body. You need to be able to load weight equally on both sides of your body, and maintain strength and speed while moving from one side to another. While there are many people who know they have an issue that compromises the body's bilateral function (a bad right hip, for example), many others are not aware that a problem with their golf game is a direct result of the right and left sides of your body operating at different levels of strength and ability. Such disparities result in golfer errors like a reverse pivot, or a weak hands-and-arms swing. Gaining bilateral function in your body is they key to a great golf game, as well as many other areas in your life. The good news is that it's never too late to gain function. Follow our Par For Life Exercise Recipes daily and on the golf course and enjoy the benefits of a healthy body.

Be kind to your spine as you finish your swing and watch your ball fly toward the hole. The very nature of a functional golf swing places your spine into a flexion and rotational position at the same time, leaving your back in a vulnerable position. As you finish your swing, transferring your weight completely to your left foot "releases" the spine and adds power to your shot. Annika Sorenstan and David Duval are two great examples of a full release. Finish upright with your weight on your left foot, and your spine, as well as your chiropractor, will thank you.

A good golf swing begins with the proper address position. The weight transfer to the right begins quickly, almost immediately as you begin your backswing. This instant loading of your weight onto the right foot allows the body to "coil" or build up tension similar to the twisting of a spring. This then enables your body to "uncoil" and explode onto the ball on the downswing. The tension created on the backswing has been labeled by many as the "X-Factor," and the exercises that Par For Life advocates to improve your own ability are the X-Factor Twist, Sitting Floor Twist and IT Band stretches. These should increase your coiling ability and strength, and give you 20 yards in 30 days.

Maintaining the tilt in your torso throughout your swing is necessary to produce a powerful, repetitive golf swing. Being able to maintain your tilt requires a lot of function through your back and hips, which is why we stress the need to do your daily exercise recipe. Using the Par For Life program to improve your body's function as well as your golf game will get one of two reactions from your chiropractor and orthopedic surgeon. Either they will be thrilled that you are taking care of your spine, or they will mourn the loss of your business!

Your grip, set-up and backswing will be the critical predictor to the success of your execution of a proper downswing, impact and finish. The body is incredibly resilient and always seeks balance. Even in the worst postures we see, people tend not to just fall down; their bodies find a way to stay upright. In the golf swing, the body reacts in the same fashion. If a golfer's weight is on their left foot at the top of the backswing (a reverse weight shift), the body will react and stay upright by transferring the weight to the right foot on the downswing. A controlled balancing action will always take place.

Though we focus on teaching our clients to work on getting the proper weight transfer back and through the swing while letting your arms and hands hang on for the ride, we would be remiss if we completely ignored the arms. Without question, the hands and arms follow the lead of the larger muscles through the golf swing. That said, they still need repetitive training to play well. A beginner develops over three to five years, and ask any seasoned golfer, the learning curve never stops. Work around the greens with pitch shots to get the feel how your arms and hands work.

Set-Up

Early Pivot

Top of Backswing

Downswing - Delay

Impact   *Release*   *Finish*

At Set-Up, the hands and arms are relaxed and tension free, forming a neutral triangle. As you take the club away, you make an Early Pivot around a steady center (your head and spine), and your hands and arms should still display a triangle at about waist high.

Continuing to the top of your backswing, your hands and arms should be parallel to each other. No matter if your swing tends to be upright or flat, all great players display parallel arms at this point in the swing.

Delay is the angle between the clubshaft and the left forearm in the downswing. Like the crack of a whip or the un-coiling of a spring, the final release of power will depend on the amount of delay you have - the smaller the angle, the more delay. At impact, the left arm leads, so that the right arm can fire like a piston.

The triangle formed between the shoulders and hands remains intact through the hit, while the hands and arms are turning over in full extension. Release is defined as the relationship between the left forearm and club shaft when your arms are about waist high. There should be about a 90° angle displayed at this point. Finally, at your finish, the hands and arms have folded over the shoulder, relaxed and free of tension.

You can barely watch a golf tournament anymore without seeing the latest gimmick or gadget that promises to forever fix your swing and improve your game. After years of playing with various swing trainers and aids, we have found that the Swing Fan continues to be the one that best produces the "picture perfect" impact position and pattern of motion through the hit. Due to the resistance the fan creates, the body has the opportunity to rotate to the left with the arms and hands lagging slightly behind, then fully extending through the hit. This sensation is common in a good golf swing, and the Swing Fan has produced consistent results in every one of our students over the years.

Swing Fan

Sides, Extras & Short Game

For our cookbook portion, we turn our sights to sides and extras. Nothing can ruin the benefits of a healthy cut of grilled salmon more than a baked potato loaded with obscene amounts of cheese, bacon and sour cream. In this section we offer healthy alternatives to fat and carb loaded side dishes without skimping on any taste.

Again, we will stress organic choices, though all of our recipes work well with non-organic foods as well. Organic vegetables, however, will be your best bet for delivering the greatest value of nutrients per serving. Naturally colorful vegetables are full of vitamins, minerals and flavanoids, and organic vegetables will give you the natural color - not the dyes and waxes designed to make inadequate vegetables look healthier.

Throughout this chapter, we will discuss the short shots, when you don't have the distance in front of you to be able to tee it high and let it fly. We'll keep it simple, and just like off of the tee, make sure your joints are in a great alignment to start with.

Some of us can hit the long ball and our short game eludes us, while others may be less than stellar off of the tee, but make up for it 100 yards and in. Wherever you lie on the spectrum, one thing is clear, you need to have a great short game if you're going improve your score.

We will also ask you to assess your posture in this chapter. Define which golfer type you fall into, and then make a commitment to yourself that every morning you will take the time to perform the appropriate recipe of exercises in order to get your joints back into a better alignment.

Player #13
Geneva National Golf Club
Lake Geneva, Wisconsin

The goal of the Par For Life Institute is to get our clients to gain function, not necessarily flexibility. Though we advocate many exercises that the flexible person may be able to do better than a non-flexible one, our aim is to get your body moving and your joints into a better alignment so that you are more functional - removing the limitations that hinder activities in your life.

For example, we ask our clients to bend over and see if they can touch their toes. Some cannot - especially athletic men with an anterior pelvic tilt. Some of them say they never could - even at their peak. While you may not need to be flexible enough to touch your toes, you do need to be functional enough to bend over and tie your shoe and get back up with ease, or get on the floor with your grandchildren without getting stuck. That's our aim - function, not necessarily flexibility.

Gaining flexibility will indeed help your golf game and improve your ability to perform other physical tasks in your life, and the exercises we prescribe should help to increase your flexibility. That being said, we truly focus on removing your physical limitations, allowing you to do all that you want to do in your life.

On the following pages we will discuss some of the functional tests that we look at in our clients to determine their base level and any problems they may show, and how we can further hone in on their postural dysfunctions to make life better.

Baked Sweet Potato Fries

4 medium sweet potatoes (about 2 pounds)
2 tablespoons plus 1 teaspoon extra virgin olive oil

¼ teaspoon sea salt
¼ teaspoon black pepper
1 ½ teaspoons sesame seeds (optional)

Preheat oven to 450°. Peel and cut sweet potatoes into ½ inch thick slices or ¾ inch thick wedges. Toss sweet potatoes with oil, salt and pepper in a large bowl.

Arrange in a single layer on a baking sheet. Roast, turning once, until tender and slightly browned, about 17 to 20 minutes. Transfer to serving dish and immediately sprinkle with sesame seeds.

Spaghetti Squash with Garlic

2 spaghetti squash (1 pound
   each)
2 tablespoons extra virgin
   olive oil

2 garlic cloves, slivered
Salt and Pepper

Preheat oven to 400°. With a fork, prick squash in several places. Place on a rimmed baking sheet and bake until soft, about 1 hour.

When cool enough to handle, halve squash crosswise. Scoop out and discard the seeds. Scrape the flesh into strands.

In a large skillet, heat olive oil over low heat. Add garlic and cook until fragrant and just starting to color, about 5 minutes. Add squash and season with salt and pepper. Cook, mixing frequently, until squash is very hot, about 5 minutes.

The pitch shot is a mini-golf swing. Unlike most other sports, golf requires the same motion for every stoke through the round; golfers do not need to master different swings where a tennis player, for example, has very different motions through a foreswing, backswing, lob or serve. While shot making, like a draw, fade or punch shot, requires skill and technique, the general motion is always the same. For every stroke of your game, you need to establish a proper set-up, transfer your weight to the right during your back swing, move your weight to the left, letting your hands and arms lag slightly behind as you follow through. For a pitch shot, we still advocate the ball placement to be in the middle of your stance as you vary the length and pace of the backswing to vary the distance.
You may notice in the far right picture that our golfer shows excessive leg movement. That tells us his hip function is lacking!

THE X-FACTOR TEST

Lie on your right side with your legs bent at 90° angles at the hips and knees. Your arms are together and straight out from your shoulders. Firmly keep your knees and feet together in this position as you bring your left arm flat to the ground on your left side as you look to your left. Hold this for one minute, then repeat on your left side. We look to see if one arm and shoulder rests closer to the floor than the other, displaying a disparity in your bilateral function. We have found the best way to get golfers to gain 20 yards in 30 days is by doing this stretch daily!

Spinach Stuffed Mushrooms

1 cup cooked spinach	4 tablespoons extra virgin olive oil
8 large mushrooms	¼ teaspoon nutmeg
1 bunch green onions, finely chopped	Sea salt and pepper to taste

Preheat the oven to 350°. Coat a glass baking dish with non-stick cooking spray.

Chop the cooled, cooked spinach then place in a strainer and press out most of the liquid.

Wash the mushrooms and remove the stems. Chop the stems finely and sauté them with the onions in the olive oil until tender. Add the spinach and cook another minute or so, mixing well, until all moisture is evaporated.

Add nutmeg and season the filling with the salt and pepper to taste. Fill the hollow of each mushroom with a spoonful of stuffing and place in the prepared glass pan. To cook, add ¼ inch water to the pan by pouring it down the sides, not on top of the mushrooms. Bake for about 20 minutes.

If you're in a hurry, you can make the filling and stuff the mushrooms ahead of time, just wait to add any water to the pan until you are ready to bake.

Baked Sweet Potato with Thyme

4 sweet potatoes (about 8
   ounces each)
$^1/_3$ cup organic vegetable broth

¼ teaspoon salt
¼ teaspoon dried thyme
Black pepper

Preheat oven to 375°. Peel sweet potatoes and cut into 1-inch cubes. In a 1 ½ quart baking dish, toss the sweet potatoes with the broth, salt, thyme, and pepper to taste.

Cover and bake for about 35 to 40 minutes, until the potatoes are tender when pierced. Serves 4.

Sweet potatoes have four times the U.S. Recommended Dietary Allowance for beta-carotene, a "pre-vitamin" that the body converts to vitamin A. Researchers are continuing to look closely at the role beta-carotene, an antioxidant, may play in cancer prevention.

Viewing the pitch shot at impact is very much like the full swing. The weight is moving to the left during the downswing. The position of the hands and arms are similar as well — slightly ahead of the ball at impact. This position will result in crisp, clean contact.
You can see on the right hand photo that in this swing, the club head was not fully released (closing). This will effect the spin, stopping the ball quickly on the green.

THE LEG LIFT

We use the Leg Lift to observe and compare the function level in each hip, and to see if both hips are functioning at the same level.

Stand with your legs hip width apart and your toes pointing forward. Lift your arms out to the side for balance. First, lift your right leg with your knee bent at a ninety degree angle as high as you can and try to hold this position for one minute. Stand straight again, then repeat with the left leg. While you are holding the stand, check your weight distribution - does it seem even on your foot, or are you balancing on your instep?

Though many of us may show some difficulty in keeping their balance, we look to see if one side seems to be more of a challenge than the other. Looking at these pictures, we have a definate problem standing on the right leg - the right ankle turns in, left shoulder drops and the left leg flares out. Unfortunately, this picture has not been contrived for the book - this body needs a Par For Life Recipe!

Grilled Artichokes with Olive Dip

6 large artichokes
1 tablespoon plus ½ teaspoon salt
2 lemons
3 cloves garlic, minced
3 tablespoons extra virgin olive oil
2 tablespoons lemon juice
¼ teaspoon black pepper

½ cup parsley, finely chopped
4 tablespoons extra virgin olive oil
2 tablespoons green olives, chopped
1 tablespoon capers, drained
1 tablespoon lemon juice
½ teaspoon Dijon mustard
¼ teaspoon black pepper

With the whole artichokes, pull off the small leaves, trim stems, snip off thorny tips, and slice tops off. In a large pot, bring 1½ inches of water to a boil. Add 1 tablespoon salt, the juice of 1 lemon, and artichokes. Cover and steam until artichoke bottoms pierce easily, about 25 to 40 minutes. While the artichokes are cooking, blend together the parsley, 4 tablespoons of olive oil, green olives, capers, 1 tablespoon lemon juice, Dijon mustard and ¼ teaspoon pepper. Set dip into refrigerator until the artichokes are ready to serve.

Drain artichokes. When cool enough to handle, cut each in half lengthwise and scrape out the fuzzy center. In a bowl, combine garlic, 3 tablespoons olive oil, 2 tablespoons lemon juice, ½ teaspoon salt, and remaining pepper. Brush artichokes with garlic mixture and set, cut side down, on a grill over medium heat. Grill, turning once, until lightly browned, 8 to 10 minutes. To serve, spoon some of the olive dip into each artichoke half, and serve the rest as a dip for the leaves.

Oven Roasted Garlic

Whole garlic bulbs
Extra virgin olive oil
Coarse black pepper
Sea salt

Preheat oven to 400°. Take a whole bulb of garlic, using a very sharp knife, cut the pointed ends off about ⅛" to ¼" deep so the flesh is exposed. Arrange the bulbs in a shallow baking dish. Drizzle a little oil evenly over each bulb. Top with pepper and a dash of sea salt. Bake uncovered for about 25 minutes or until soft and golden. Remove for the oven and turn cooked bulbs over flesh side down in dish for 10 minutes to absorb the oil.

Squeeze soft garlic out of skins and spread on meat or breads or add to your favorite salads.

The finish position of any golf swing typically illustrates how well the elements of the rest of the swing were performed. The pitch shot is no exception. If you want to pitch well, make a mini golf swing allowing your weight to transfer to your right and back through to your left with the ball in the middle of your stance, just as you would with a full swing.

Heart disease may run in your family, and that is certainly a prime risk factor for you, but there are a variety of other factors you should look at as well.

Understanding your levels of Homocysteine, C-Reactive Protein, Fibrinogen, and Cholesterol will give you and your doctor a good understanding of your individual status. When you look at cholesterol, get a full lipoprotein test including, LDL particle, Small LDL, HDL, LDL, triglycerides, VLDL and Lipoprotein (a) levels.

TOUCH YOUR TOES

It sounds so simple, yet so many people, even talented athletes, have trouble touching their toes. We ask our clients to bend over and touch their toes so that we can evaluate both their hip function and general tightness.

To test yourself, first, with your feet hip width apart and your knees straight, bend over and touch your toes. Can you? Now stand back up. Get your feet hip width apart with your feet both pointed straight forward. Stand up and feel a nice, natural s-curve in your back.

Now bend forward again, but only from your hips, without arching your back in any way. How far do you get this way?

When we find a client who has difficulty bending from the hips, their first reaction is often to say that they have always had tight hamstrings. While this may be true, we will not only work to address their hamstrings, but truly focus on their hips that are causing the tightness.

For men, there is one important blood test that should not be missed. The PSA test shows the levels of the Prostate Specific Antigen, a protein made by the prostate gland. Elevated PSA levels may indicate inflammation, enlargement or prostate cancer. Whether you currently know your levels or not, one thing is clear – herbs like saw palmetto promote prostate health, and any man over thirty should look into adding them to his regimen.

Mel's Salsa

6 medium ripe tomatoes, chopped
2 bunches green onions, chopped including green part
2 bunches cilantro
1 jalapeno peppers, ends cut off
1 serrano pepper, ends cut off
1 large clove garlic
Fresh juice of one lime
½ cup water
1 8 oz can tomato sauce

Chop the tomatoes, green onions and 1 bunch cilantro and mix together in a large bowl.

In a blender, combine 1 bunch cilantro, garlic, water, peppers, and lime juice. For a milder salsa, remove the seeds from the peppers prior to blending.

Spoon blended mixture into the chopped mixture. Add more or less of the blended mix depending on the consistency and how spicy you prefer (the blended mixture adds the spiciness).

Add ½ can tomato sauce. Add more or less depending on taste and desired chunkiness. Serve with unsalted organic blue corn chips. Salsa is excellent as a topping or a dip. It can also be used to perk up dishes from scrambled eggs to grilled chicken. Make it several hours in advance to allow its flavors to blend.

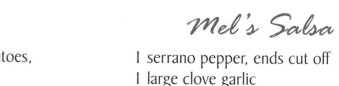

Green Beans with Water Chestnuts

1 ½ pounds fresh green beans
1 ½ teaspoons extra virgin olive oil
1 8 ounce can diced water
   chestnuts, rinsed and drained

1 teaspoon hot-pepper oil
1 tablespoon sesame seeds,
   dry-roasted

In a large saucepan over high heat, bring to a boil enough water to cover the beans. Meanwhile, trim the beans and cut into 1 ½ inch pieces. Boil for 4 minutes. Remove from pan and plunge into ice water to stop the cooking process. Drain.

Heat a large skillet over high heat. Pour both oils into the skillet and swirl to coat. Heat the water chestnuts for 1 minute, stirring constantly. Stir in the sesame seeds and beans. Cook until heated through, stirring constantly.

We use the chip shot around the green when we need to be very accurate and distance is not the priority. In a chip shot, DO NOT allow your wrist to hinge or otherwise break. Set up your weight just slightly toward your forward foot. Place your feet so that the golf ball in either is the middle of your stance or one golf ball width back of center. You are now ready to go, and the stroke is made with an arm and shoulder swing.

What ruins a fat? Exposure to light, heat, and air makes oils and fats turn rancid. When cooking with oil, use a quality extra virgin olive oil. First pressed or cold pressed olive oils mean the same thing. Anything else should be left on the shelves. Many inferior oils are expelled by chemical inducement, and that is not good for human consumption. Store your oils well sealed in a cool, dry and dark place to keep it fresh.

Sweet & Spicy Almonds

6 cups whole raw almonds	2 teaspoons salt
2 cups raw pumpkin seeds	$^3/_4$ cup Splenda®
2 teaspoons cajun spice mix	$^1/_2$ cup trans fat free margarine
1 teaspoon ground cumin	$^3/_4$ cup pure maple syrup

Preheat the oven to 375°.

In a large saucepan, combine the nuts, seeds, Splenda® and margarine together and mix well, until the Splenda® and margarine have melted. Add the maple syrup and stir until all of the nuts and seeds are well coated.

Continue to heat until bubbly. Remove from the pan and spread evenly on a baking sheet. Mix the spices together well, and sprinkle evenly over the coated nuts and seeds.

Place in the oven and toast for 10 to 15 minutes. Turn the nuts over and return to the oven for another 15 minutes until the mix appears dry. Set aside to cool before serving. The nuts will keep for up to two weeks if kept in a well sealed container.

Now we get down to it... WHAT ARE YOU? Are you an "In the Rough" with your toes pointed outward and your hips tilted forward? Are you a "Need Greens in Regulation" with your hips pointed back and working toward a c-curve in your spine? Are you a "Out of Bounds" with elevations and rotations? Or are you a combination of two?

Have a friend take four full body pictures of you - make sure you can see your knees and try to see your waistline. You should look at one head-on, one from the back, and one from each side. Posture photos tend to be mug-shots, so don't worry about looking good! Reviewing the pictures, you can decide which body type you are. If you need help, upload your photos to our website at www.ParForLife.com.

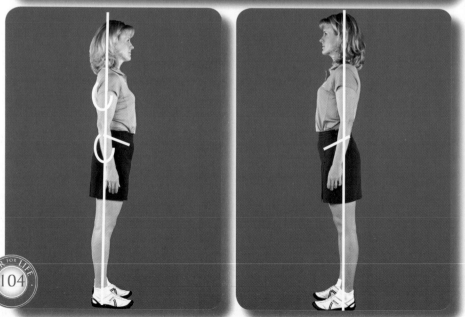

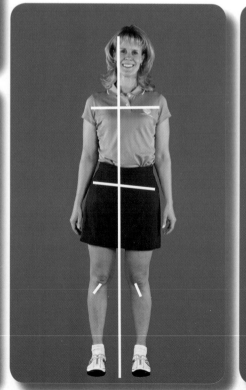

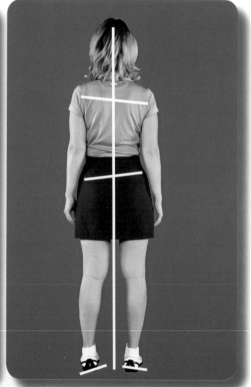

Broccoli with Garlic Butter & Cashews

1 ½ pound broccoli,
    cut into bite size pieces
$\frac{1}{3}$ cup trans fat free margarine
3 tablespoons brown sugar-
    Splenda® blend
3 tablespoons low sodium soy
    sauce

2 teaspoons white vinegar
¼ teaspoon black pepper
2 cloves garlic, chopped
$\frac{1}{3}$ cup cashews, chopped

Steam broccoli, then arrange on serving platter. While broccoli is cooking, melt margarine in a small skillet over medium heat. Mix brown sugar, soy sauce, vinegar, pepper and garlic. Bring to a boil, remove from heat. Mix in cashews and pour the sauce over the broccoli.

One of the major benefits of cross training is the prevention of injury by repetitive motion. We use caution with that term, however, because repetitive motion on its own is not dangerous - repeating an improper motion with a misaligned joint is the problem.
That being said, by changing up your routine, you work your muscles and joints differently than the day before, creating strength and function throughout the body. Besides the physical benefits, cross training prevents exercise burn-out.

After establishing the fundamental set-up, the backswing of the chip shot is basically an arm and shoulder swing to the right. It is the pace, length and club selection that then dictates how far your chip will go. Practice with different club selections, vary your pace and length of your arm swing so you know how to make the shot on the course.

IN THE ROUGH EXERCISE RECIPE

If your self-assessment has brought you to the conclusion that you have an anterior pelvic tilt, then you are an "IN THE ROUGH" Golfer. Most likely, your illiopsoas muscle, the main muscle that connects your upper body to your lower body, is overly tight, causing your lumbar spine to become closer to the front of your femur, thus pulling your pelvis forward. This deviation from the body's design ultimately leads to other compensating deviations. This Recipe is designed to get your pelvis back into a more neutral position.

1 - Back Settle. Relax for 5 Minutes
2 - Standing Shoulder Shrugs - 30 repetitions
3 - Back Settle Reverse Presses - 30 repetitions
4 - Standing Shoulder Rolls - 30 repetitions each, forward and back
5 - Standing Arm Circles - 40 repetitions each, forward and back
6 - Back Settle Pullovers - 30 repetitions
7 - Lay Back Gluteal Contractions - 60 repetitions
8 - Lay Back Knee Pillow Squeezes - 60 repetitions
9 - Foot Circles, Point & Flexes - 40 repetitions each direction
10 - Supine Groin Stretch - 15 minutes per side
11 - Wall Sit - 2 minutes

This should take you about 45 minutes, and is best done in the morning. If that's too much time, do exercises 1-9 and 11 in the morning, and save the Supine Groin Stretch for the evening.

Please refer to pages 128 for complete instructions.

Fresh or Frozen? When we hear a statement that frozen fruit and vegetables are just as good for you as fresh fruit and vegetables, we feel that someone lacks the basic understanding of life force. Let's take a look at what that means. The sun shines down on the produce giving it life and energy to sustain life. When that produce is taken out of the ground and consumed relatively quickly, that energy is transferred into the body. Produce and fruit that is picked, shipped, shelved, and frozen lacks that beneficial life force. Don't be fooled or convinced to the contrary. Organic and fresh is best.

Guacamole

2 large ripe avocados, peeled and diced
1 small red onion, diced, about ¾ cup
1 garlic clove, minced
½ cup tomatoes, seeded, diced and drained
¼ cup cilantro, chopped
2 tablespoons lime juice
1 teaspoon jalapeno pepper, minced and seeded
1 ½ teaspoons taco seasoning
¼ teaspoon Tabasco® sauce
½ teaspoon Worcestershire sauce

Mash together avocados, onion and garlic. Mix in tomato, cilantro and jalapeno. Add in lime juice, seasoning and Tabasco® sauce. Cover and refrigerate 30 minutes.

Serve with organic blue corn tortilla chips. Makes about 2 cups.

Orzo Salad

1 pound orzo pasta, uncooked
2 small tomatoes, chopped
1 small red onion, minced
¼ cup black olives, chopped
1 small pickling cucumber,
    peeled and diced
Salt to taste

6 oz reduced fat feta cheese,
    crumbled
⅓ cup dill, either fresh or
    dried
¼ cup extra virgin olive oil
¼ cup red wine vinegar

In a large pot, bring 2 quarts of water to a vigorous boil.

Cook pasta in rapidly boiling water until slightly al dente (about 8-10 minutes). Drain the pasta and transfer to a bowl. Toss pasta with the olive oil. Add the vinegar, tomatoes, onion, olives, cucumber, salt and dill. Toss well and top with feta cheese. Can be served at either room temperature or chilled. Serve by itself, on a bed of fresh greens or with cold, cubed chicken.

Today people readily believe that as you age your eyesight will deteriorate and that macular degeneration and cataracts are simply a fact of aging. This does not need to be the case. Eat foods high in carotenoids, keep your inflammation down, and consider taking supplements of two carotenoids directly contributing to eye health, lutein and zeaxanthin. Other supplements such as Ginko Biloba, N-Acetyl Carnosine, and L-Carnosine have shown promise in promoting eye health. Check with your doctor before starting on any new supplements, and start paying attention to your eye health so you can track your ball down the fairway into old age.

If you watch golf on television, and of course you do – we all do - notice the finish position of the tour professional's chip shots. Their hands stay ahead of the clubface during and after the shot. If you want to become a good chipper, always-always-always keep your hands ahead of the clubface during the chip swing.

Homemade Chunky Applesauce

4 apples, preferably golden
  delicious, granny smith,
  gala, or Rome beauty
½ cup frozen organic apple
  juice concentrate

½ cup water
Seasoning of your preference:
  cinnamon, vanilla, ginger
  or cardamon

Peel, quarter, and core the apples. Dice into ¾-inch pieces. Put apples, apple juice concentrate, and ½ cup water in a large sauce-pan. Bring to a simmer over moderate heat, cover, and adjust heat to maintain a gentle simmer. Cook until apples are tender, about 6 minutes. Transfer mixture to a food processor and pulse to achieve desired consistency. Serve warm or cold. You can flavor this basic applesauce however you like: with a little vanilla, cinnamon, ginger, or cardamon.

OUT OF BOUNDS EXERCISE RECIPE

If your self evaluation reveals that you have elevations and rotations in your joints, but your pelvis is in a fairly neutral position, you are in our second category of golfers. This exercise recipe is designed to reduce the disparities in your posture, and get your right and left sides working together to restore the bilateral function of your body's design.

1 - Back Settle - Relax for 5 minutes
2 - Standing Windmill - 10 repetitions of 4 positions
3 - Gravity Drop - Hold for 3 minutes
4 - Pelvic Tilts - 10 repetitions foward and back
5 - Lay Back Gluteal Contractions - 60 repetitions
6 - Lay Back Knee Pillow Squeezes - 60 repetitions
7 - Foot Circles & Point-Flexes - 40 repetitions each
8 - X-Factor Twist - Hold for 2 minutes each side
9 - Wall Sit - Hold for 2 minutes

This recipe should take about 20 minutes. For complete instructions for every exercise, please refer to the section at the end of this book.

Annual evaluation of a blood Hormone Panel will give you a glimpse at the overall working of your endocrine system. Proper function of your hormones and glands has much more impact on one's longevity than just hot flashes and sex drive. Keeping healthy hormone levels is essential to many vital systems in our bodies and a key to retaining muscle mass into old age, not to mention the cosmetic effects of youthful skin and maintaining lean body mass over fat stores. If you are still in your twenties or thirties, be sure not to wait until you feel the effects of aging. Get a complete Hormone Panel when you feel young and great – in ten or twenty years, it will help you and your doctors know what your ideal levels looked like.

Has your metabolism changed over the years? Many of ours do with age, but if you experience a sudden change, your thoughts should turn to your Thyroid. When you ask your doctor for your annual blood testing, be sure to include a Thyroid Panel, indicating the gland's function and balance. When Thyroid levels fall above or below the norm, you and your doctor should talk.

Green Beans & Almonds

1 ½ pounds string beans,
    French cut

2 tablespoons trans fat free
    margarine

²/₃ cup crispy organic almond
    slivers

Steam beans about 2 to 3 minutes. Melt the margarine in a skillet, raise heat, add the almonds and cook, stirring, until lightly browned. Be careful not to burn. Toss with the beans and keep warm in the oven, covered until ready to serve. Serves 6

Testing for DHEA levels in your bloodstream is another value reading that you should annually ask your doctor to review. DHEA is the abbreviation for Dehyroepiandrosterone, a hormone produced by the adrenal glands that is a component of the hormonal cascade providing for the building blocks of testosterone. Though known as a male hormone, women need testosterone as well to stay healthy and strong. This supplement is readily available, but, men especially, we strongly caution you not to take this without knowing your blood chemistry, especially your PSA levels. In an unhealthy prostate, extra DHEA can feed cancer cells and make PSA levels skyrocket!

Even though your weight starts slightly on the left foot, a mini weight transfer will still take place at impact in the chip shot. The weight continues to move left as the hands and arms swing forward. As the hands and arms start, they remain slightly forward of the ball, resulting in a descending blow.

Roasted Asparagus

2 pounds fresh asparagus,
    trimmed
¼ cup melted trans fat free
    margarine

3 green onions, chopped
½ teaspoon salt (optional)

Place asparagus in a shallow baking dish coated with nonstick cooking spray. Combine the margarine and green onions; spoon over asparagus. Sprinkle with salt. Bake, uncovered, at 425° for 10-15 minutes or until lightly browned. Serves 6

NEED GREENS IN REGULATIONS EXERCISE RECIPE

If your self assessment has revealed that your pelvis shows a posterior pelvic tilt, you are in our third category of golfers. Traditionally a posterior tilt would indicate weakness - a sign of aging and "natural" body decay. We no longer take this view. True, aging and weakness will allow the pelvis to tilt under and the spine to curve forward. We find, however, that many strong athletes, including bicyclists, runners and pilates experts, put their low back and pelvis in a flexed position so often, that they develop a posterior tilt out of strength.

The following recipe is designed to return the posterior pelvis to a more neutral position:

1 - Standing Shoulder Rolls - 30 repetitions forward and back
2 - Standing Arm Circles - 40 repetitions forward and back
3 - Static Extension Position - Hold for 1 minute
4 - Lay Back Gluteal Contractions - 60 repetitions
5 - Back Settle Reverse Presses - 30 repetitions
6 - Lay Back Knee Pillow Squeezes - 60 repetitions
7 - Lay Back Isolated Hip Flexor Lifts - 60 repetitions each side
8 - Supine Gluteal Contractions - 60 repetitions
9 - Foot Circles & Point-Flexes - 40 repetitions each
10 - Supine Groin with Towels - Relax for 15 Minutes
11 - Wall Sit- Hold for 2 minutes

For complete instructions, please go to page 138.

    This recipe should take you about 45 minutes.

Spicy Sweet Corn

4 large ears of sweet corn
2 tablespoons extra virgin
   olive oil
1 tablespoon trans fat free
   margarine

1 jalapeno pepper, seeded and
   minced
$^1/_2$ teaspoon ground cumin
$^1/_4$ teaspoon pepper

Fill a large saucepan half full of water and bring to a boil. Add corn; cover and cook 5-7 minutes or until tender.

Meanwhile, in a small saucepan, heat oil and margarine over low heat until melted. Stir in the jalapeno, cumin and pepper. Drain corn; brush with the margarine mixture and serve while hot.

Bunker shots tend to get golfers flustered. Keep it simple and enjoy your time in the sand. For a greenside bunker, choose a club with a great amount of loft, and place the ball about three inches ahead of the center line of your set-up, closer to your front foot. Your swing itself is the same as we have discussed throughout the book, the only difference being that rather than striking the ball directly, strike the sand 2 to 3 inches behind the ball, and allow the sand to throw the golf ball out of the bunker and on to the green.

Palmer #8
Geneva National Golf Club, Lake Geneva, Wisconsin

Desserts & Putting

What's life without sweets? The Par For Life Institute advocates living life to the fullest, and a great chocolate brownie is certainly a part of that! With that in mind, we all still need to be careful to keep our protein and fiber levels up while not spiking our insulin.

So many store-bought "low-fat" baked goods taste awful because of all the chemicals and stabilizers added for a longer shelf life. The truth is, longevity is for people, not baked goods. If you can take 15 minutes plus some oven time to make your own treats, you can trick your sweet tooth into adding healthy protein and fiber to your daily sugar fix.

The dessert recipes that follow are decadent, delicious treats that keep our Front Nine principles at the highest priority. Instead of white flour with no nutritional value, we use whole wheat. Instead of refined white sugar, we use sucralose (Splenda®) which is readily available at supermarkets and does not break down to leave a chemical signature in your body like other artificial sweeteners. In addition, when it does not compromise the taste and texture, we add freshly ground flaxseeds or whey protein powder.

Try out these recipes, and then take our lead in modifying your own favorites. You may need to use less sucralose than sugar, depending on the type you purchase. You may need to add extra moisture to a batter when you use whole wheat flour and other whole grain alternatives. Try substituting oil, and especially shortening, with unsweetened apple sauce, nonfat yogurt or rehydrated dried fruit. If you take the time to play with your old favorite recipes, you will, no doubt, find a new, exciting and heathy favorite.

A warning to parents & grandparents: don't tell your kids these are healthy - they'll never know & gobble up the treats!

Player #6
Geneva National Golf Club
Lake Geneva, Wisconsin

Berry Berry Cake

$^1/_3$ cup light cream cheese
$^3/_4$ cup plus 2 tablespoons Splenda®
2 egg whites
2 teaspoons grated fresh lemon peel

1 cup plus 2 tablespoons whole wheat pastry flour
$^1/_2$ teaspoon baking soda
$^1/_3$ cup fat free sour cream
3 cups of mixed berries

Preheat oven to 350°. Coat a 9-inch springform pan with nonstick cooking spray.

Beat together the cream cheese and $^1/_2$ cup of the Splenda® until well blended. Add the egg whites and lemon peel and mix well.

Sift together 1 cup of the flour and the baking soda. Add this to the cream cheese mixture alternately with the sour cream. Mix well between each addition.

Spread the batter into the bottom of the coated pan and 1 inch up the sides. Toss the berries with the 2 tablespoons Splenda® and flour, then spoon into the middle of the batter, leaving about $^1/_2$ inch around all sides free of berries.

Bake for 40 to 45 minutes until a toothpick inserted in the center comes out clean, Cool for 10 minutes before removing the sides of the pan. Top with the remaining berries and serve alone or with ice cream.

The exercise recipes in the previous section are a great way to start your day, and we certainly advocate doing your routine first thing in the morning. The recipes are designed to get your body back into a better alignment, and you'll feel great if that's the way you start your day.

That being said, if you find that you tend to stiffen up mid-round on the golf course, we certainly don't want you to wait until the next morning to stretch things out. Many of the standing exercises you can do right on the course - and this section will show you a couple of our on-course favorites.

Baking with Whole Wheat flour can be tricky... here's the secret: DON'T SKIP THE SIFTING, and measure the flour after you sift it. One cup of unsifted flour, once sifted, fills about one and a half cups! Take your time & make it right.

If you are modifying your own recipe, you may need to use less whole wheat flour than you would all-purpose. For more delicate recipes, you may trying only half whole wheat, and half all purpose flour.

Marinated Strawberries

2 pints strawberries, hulled and
   sliced in half
¼ cup balsamic vinegar
1 teaspoon Stevia or
   2 teaspoons Splenda®

1 ½ teaspoons vanilla extract
½ teaspoon orange zest
1 32 oz container plain organic
   non-fat yogurt, drained
4 mint leaves, chopped

Place strawberries in a large bowl, mix in Stevia or Splenda® and balsamic vinegar. Refrigerate, and allow to marinate 30 minutes to 2 hours.

Mix vanilla extract and orange zest with yogurt. Place a dollop of yogurt mixture in 4 bowls and top with the strawberries and balsamic juice. Garnish with mint. Serves 4

At the Par For Life Institute, we advocate two sweeteners: Sucralose (Splenda®) and stevia, most importantly because they do not effect your insulin levels like sugar and fructose, and they exit your body without leaving chemical markers like aspartame and other artificial sweeteners do.

Splenda® is readily available in grocery stores, and also comes in a Brown Sugar blend. Use a cup of Splenda® for a cup of sugar, and half as much with the brown sugar blend.

Please see page 32 for information on stevia, a very sweet natural herb available in most health food stores. Stevia is a little trickier to use than Splenda®, one teaspoon is enough for a dozen cookies, so adjusting your favorite recipe for stevia does take practice.

The 20-foot putt is just as important to your score as your tee shot, although it doesn't always feel that way. Proper set-up mechanics, feel and club fit all play and important role in becoming a good putter. To begin our discussion on putting, we focus on a neutral set-up. From the front view, shoulders over hips over knees over ankles, with your hands positioned down the center line, as well as the ball.

Warm Apple Crisp

6 apples, preferably Rome beauty or golden delicious

2 tablespoons apple juice concentrate

1 tablespoon Splenda®

1 tablespoon cornstarch

2 teaspoons lemon juice

2 cups water

½ teaspoon cinnamon

Crisp Topping:

⅔ cup rolled oats

⅓ cup Grape-Nuts® cereal

1 tablespoon peach jam

Preheat oven to 375°. Peel, core, and quarter the apples. Cut them into ½-inch pieces. In a large saucepan, combine apples, apple juice concentrate, Splenda®, cornstarch, lemon juice, cinnamon, and water. Bring to a simmer over moderate heat, adjust heat to maintain a simmer and cook for 15 minutes. The syrup should thicken slightly and fall below the level of the apples.

To make the crisp topping, combine Grape-Nuts®, jam and all but 1 tablespoon of the oats in a food processor and process until jam is evenly distributed and mixture has a streusel-like feel. Transfer to a bowl and stir in the reserved 1 tablespoon rolled oats.

Transfer the apples to a 9-inch pie pan. Spread the crisp topping evenly over the apples, pressing it lightly into place. Bake until apples are bubbly and topping is lightly browned, about 25 minutes.

STANDING or SITTING CATS & DOGS

So much of the golf swing is rotational movement, and we find that nothing feels better mid-round than to get a full front to back range of motion going. Cats & Dogs is the perfect exercise, but you may get too many strange looks on the course if you get on all fours.

Instead, from a standing position, bend your knees a little, and tilt your torso slightly forward. With your hands on your knees and your weight forward, stretch your lower back out, and push your shoulders away from your knees, rounding your upper back up and dropping your head forward. That's the cat. Now look up, pinch your shoulder blades together and draw your shoulders back as you roll your pelvis forward, creating a big arch in your low back. That's the dog. You can also do this sitting in the golf cart, as pictured above, though you don't get as much hip motion.

Paper Thin Fruit Pies

1 medium apple, cored and thinly sliced

1 medium ripe pear, cored and thinly sliced

2 tablespoons lemon juice

2 ounces trans fat free margarine

4 rectangular sheets of phyllo pastry, thawed if frozen

2 tablespoons low-sugar apricot preserves

1 tablespoon fresh squeezed orange juice

2 teaspoons powdered sugar, for dusting

Preheat the oven to 400°. Core and thinly slice the apple and pear and toss them in lemon juice to prevent discoloration. Gently melt the margarine in a pan set over low heat. Cut each sheet of pastry into 4 pieces and cover with a clean, damp dish cloth, making 16 sheets of pastry in total. Coat 4 spots of a jumbo muffin tin with nonstick cooking spray and fill the remaining spots with a little water.

Working on each pie separately, brush 4 sheets of pastry with melted margarine. Press a small sheet of pastry into the base of one large muffin spot. Arrange the other sheets of pastry on top at slightly different angles. Repeat with the other sheets of pastry to make another 3 pies.

Arrange the apple and pear slices alternately in the center of each pastry case and lightly crimp the edges of the pastry of each pie. Mix the preserve and orange juice together until smooth and brush over the fruit. Bake for 12-15 minutes. Dust lightly with the powdered sugar. Serves 4. You can make the pies ahead of time and refrigerate, but take care to let the pies warm back to room temperature prior to baking.

Got the Yips? Try the Heartmath Program. Heartmath focuses on teaching golfers how to maintain a balanced emotional state. In other words, staying calm and not letting your nerves get to you on the course. When it comes to putting, we've achieved tremendous success with the program. It's easy to learn, and worth the time. Go to www.heartmath.com for more details.

From the side view, several alignments should be maintained at your address position and through the putt. Your hands should fall through an imaginary vertical line which bisects the shoulder. This alignment places the hands in a very stable, strong position relative to the stroke. Your eyes should look directly over the ball, dictated by the amount of tilt in your hips. If you have trouble seeing the line of the putt, increase or decrease your tilt while maintaining the position of your eye over the ball until you can see the line better.

A little bit of the right dessert after dinner hits the spot. So does a little professional bodywork after a couple of weeks working out. Who doesn't love a good massage? While a traditional Swedish massage can be relaxing, our preference for bodywork is Rolfing or Hellerwork. These practitioners realign the body by using pressure and stroking to stretch shortened and tightened fascia back into shape. We have experienced incredible results with these protocols in conjunction with the functional exercise we recommend. If you find a practitioner near you, don't expect a day at the spa. These are trained professionals aiming to work your body into a better alignment. Check out these web sites, www.rolfing.com and www.hellerwork.com, to do your homework and find an experienced practitioner in your area.

Almond Oat Chocolate Chip Cookies

1 ½ cup whole wheat pastry flour
¾ teaspoon baking powder
½ teaspoon salt
½ cup trans fat free margarine
½ cup organic almond butter
1 cup Splenda®

2 teaspoons pure vanilla extract
2 large egg whites
1 cup rolled oats
¾ cup organic dark chocolate chips

Preheat the oven to 375°. Sift the flour, baking powder and salt and set aside. Mix the margarine, Splenda® and vanilla and beat until creamy. Add the egg and mix well. Add the almond butter and mix well. Stir in the flour a little at a time until well mixed. Add the oats and chocolate chips and stir all together.

Drop rounded tablespoons of the batter onto cookie sheets about 2 inches apart. Gently flatten the cookies. Bake for about 10 or 12 minutes, until golden brown. Remove from the pan and cool on a rack. Makes about 2 dozen cookies.

SITTING TWIST

Somtimes with all of that deliberate twisting in the golf swing, a twisitng stretch feels great. As you are sitting in your cart, take care to keep your lower body stable and still. Take your right arm and put it on the top/back of your cart bench. Take your left hand and place it on the outside of your right knee. Now look over your right shoulder, and twist to your right as far as you can. Hold it for a minute and get a good stretch before repeating on your left side.

Sugar-Free Brownies

½ cup organic brown rice syrup
1 tablespoon trans fat free
    margarine
1 square unsweetened baking
    chocolate (1 ounce)

1 teaspoon vanilla
3 egg whites
½ cup sifted whole wheat
    pastry flour
½ cup chopped pecan or walnuts

Preheat oven to 350°. In a medium saucepan, melt margarine and choc-olate on low heat. Thoroughly stir in brown rice syrup and remove from heat. Blend in egg whites slowly and add vanilla. Stir in flour and add nuts, if desired.

Spread in a greased 8x8 inch baking pan. Bake for 30 minutes or un-til a knife comes out clean. Cool on a wire rack. When cool, cut into squares.

For your backstroke, the putting motion is generated from the rotation of the shoulders and movement of the arms with a light yet firm grip on the putter, swinging the club in a pendulum mo-tion back and through the putt in equal lengths.
The legendary Paul Ruyan favored an opposing putting grip (left hand lower than the right) for its stability of clubhead movement. Though it may feel a little odd, try it a couple of times on the prac-tice green. It may give you the edge you've been looking for.

SPREAD FOOT FOWARD BEND

To really stretch your hamstrings and lower back in the middle of your round, move to the front of your cart and face the windshield. Place your feet in a very wide stance, and make sure your toes are pointed straight forward. Stand up straight, still facing your cart, and make sure you have a nice, neutral s-curve in your back. Now bend forward from your hips only, keeping your back in this neutral position. Only bend forward as far as you can without curving your back out of this position. Place your hands on the cart for support, and hold for one minute. Keep working and bending further from the pelvis, not from the back. After one minute, try walking your hands to the left and holding it for another minute, then the right.

Chewy Date Bars

3/4 cup whole wheat pastry flour
1 cup oats
1/2 cup brown sugar-Splenda® blend
1/4 teaspoon baking soda

3/4 cup trans fat free margarine
2 cups whole, unsweetened dates
2 cups water
1 lemon

Preheat oven to 350°. Place water and dates in a medium saucepan and bring to a boil. Lower heat, cover and simmer, stirring frequently, until dates turn to a mush, usually about 15-20 minutes. Remove from heat and add the juice of one lemon.

While the dates are cooking, sift the flour into a mixing bowl and add all of the other dry ingredients. Melt the margarine, and mix with the dry ingredients into a flaky batter.

Grease an 8x8 baking dish and press half of the batter into the bottom. Smooth the dates over the batter, and place the remaining batter on top of the dates. Bake for 30 minutes until golden brown, and allow to cool completely before cutting and serving.

Chocolate Bundt Cake

1¾ cup whole wheat pastry flour
½ cup unsweetened cocoa
   powder
1⅔ cup Splenda®
1¾ teaspoons bakng soda
⅛ teaspoon salt

½ cup trans fat free margarine
3 tablespoons organic skim milk
1 teaspoon pure vanilla extract
¼ cup water
2 eggs
2 egg whites

Preheat oven to 350°. Coat a 12-cup bundt pan with nonstick cooking spray and lightly dust the pan with flour.

Combine all of the dry ingredients together and set aside.

Combine the margarine, vanilla, milk, eggs and water together and whisk together until creamy. Add the wet ingredients to the dry ingredients and beat on a medium speed until well mixed, 3 or 4 minutes.

Pour the batter into the bundt pan. Bake for 35 to 40 minutes, until an inserted toothpick comes out clean. Allow to cool completely in the pan before turning it onto a serving platter. Serve plain, add fresh raspberries, with a simple icing or with low-fat frozen yogurt.

The pendulum motion of your putting should move your putter back and through the stroke in equal lengths, with a slight acceleration forward. Practice makes permanent – so get it right. As always, address the ball in a balanced and functional position as you work on your pace and feel.

Cinnamon is probably one of the most popular and recognized spices on the shelf, and can be used for every meal – sweet or savory. Not only is it tasty, cinnamon has long been recognized for its health benefits, including anti-clotting action, anti-microbial activity, anti-inflamatory properties, blood-sugar controlling properties and its assistance in boosting brain function. Make sure your cinnamon smells sweet to ensure freshness.

GOLF GRAVITY DROP

Stand in back of your cart on the platform that holds your bags, with the balls of your feet on the cart and your heels off. Hold on to the roof of the cart for support, and try to make sure that you are standing straight - not leaning forward or back. Now drop your heels, and feel the stretch through the back of your legs. Keep your body in a straight line, and hold this for one minute.

Carrot Cake

3 egg whites
¼ cup Splenda®
½ cup unsweetened organic applesauce
½ cup fat-free organic plain yogurt
¼ cup brown sugar-Splenda® blend

1 tablespoon extra virgin olive oil
2 cups whole wheat pastry flour
1 ½ cups grated carrots
¼ cup chopped walnuts (optional)
½ tablespoon ground cinnamon
1 teaspoon baking soda

Preheat oven to 350°. Lightly spray an 8-inch square cake pan with non-stick cooking spray.

In a large bowl, whisk together the egg substitute, Splenda®, applesauce, yogurt, brown sugar and olive oil.

In another large bowl, whisk together the remaining ingredients. Add to the liquid mixture and whisk until combined. Do not over mix. Pour the batter into the cake pan.

Bake for 30 to 35 minutes, or until a tooth pick inserted in the center comes out clean. Serves 12

For an easy Cream Cheese Frosting, beat together 8 ounces reduced fat cream cheese and 1 tablespoon Splenda® until smooth and creamy. Spread evenly over cake surface.

Chewy Chocolate Brownies

1 cup whole wheat pastry flour
1 cup Splenda®
1/2 cup unsweetened cocoa
   powder
1/2 teaspoon baking soda
1/2 teaspoon baking powder
1/4 teaspoon cinnamon

1/3 cup softened trans fat free
   margarine
2 teaspoons pure almond extract
2 large eggs
1 large egg white
2/3 cup organic chocolate chips

Preheat the oven to 325°. Spray a 8x8 inch baking pan with non-stick cooking spray and line with parchment paper.

Mix together all of the dry ingredients - flour, Splenda®, cocoa powder, baking soda, baking powder, & cinnamon. Add the margarine and stir until the mixture is coarse and crumbly. Add the vanilla and eggs and mix until the batter is moist. Fold in the chocolate chips.

Spread the batter into the baking pan in one even layer. Bake for about 20 minutes, or until a toothpick inserted in the center comes out clean. Let cool in the pan. When cool, cut into squares just shy of 2 inches and store in an airtight container. Makes about 18 brownies.

Though you need to practice your fundamentals to make the proper putting stroke, you also need to choose your putter wisely. The loft on your putter should launch the ball laterally until gravity takes over, and only then does the ball start to roll. Essentially, in a good putt the ball first skids along the green three or four inches before it rolls toward the hole. Too much or too little loft will cause the ball to either bounce or spin, making your putts inconsistent at best.

To summarize our exercise goals for every golfer, we want you to stay strong and limber throughout your life, so that the aches and pains of aging have little effect on your daily activities. We all strive to be able to make Par For Life, and keeping your body in the best alignment possible is your surest bet to stay active without limitations.

In this book we have provided very general exercise recipes for three basic types of golfers. Our hope is that you integrate these recipes into your daily life, and realize the benefits of a better aligned body.

Keep in mind that these recipes are very general, and though you should see positive results, a true personal assessment will serve you better than this book. Having a recipe created just for you will take into account your individual posture as well as your specific limitations, aches and pains, strength, time restrictions and goals. The Par For Life Institute is equipped to deliver a personal recipe, either in person by visiting our Lake Geneva, Wisconsin facility, or through our website by uploading four pictures of your posture along with some related information. Log on to our website at www.ParForLife.com for information on how to receive your personal assessment, and also for updated information on golf, exercise, strength training and nutrition. We'll keep you informed, so that we can see you on the tee for many years, and challenge you to shoot your age at 80 and beyond.

Thank you, and be sure to make Par For Life!

Baked Cinnamon Pears

4 ripe pears
2 tablespoons fresh squeezed
   lemon juice
4 tablespoons brown sugar-
   Splenda® blend

1 teaspoon ground cinnamon
¼ cup trans fat free margarine
finely sliced lemon zest for garnish

Preheat the oven to 400°. Peel the pears, slice them in half lengthwise and remove the cores. Brush them all over with the lemon juice. Place the pears, core side down, in a large enough nonstick baking dish. Take care to find a dish that fits all eight halves comfortably without too much extra room.

In a small sauce pan, heat the brown sugar, cinnamon and margarine. Heat gently, stirring all the while until the sugar dissolves. Keep the heat low in order to maintain the moisture levels. When the sugar is melted, spoon the mixture evenly over the pears.

Bake for 20-25 minutes, spooning the liquid and sugar on top of the pears occasionally. When finished, the pears should be tender and golden brown. Remove the pears from the oven. Arrange two pear halves on each plate and garnish with the lemon zest. Serves 4.

As an option, these pears are wonderful served with lowfat vanilla custard-style yogurt. Quickly heat up the yogurt, and spoon one tablespoon full on a plate, then place the pears on top.

Blueberry Torte

1 cup whole wheat pastry flour
½ cup all-purpose flour
1 ½ teaspoons baking powder
3 cups fresh blueberries
1 tablespoon trans fat free
   margarine
¼ cup extra virgin olive oil
½ teaspoon cinnamon
2 tablespoons cornstarch
½ cup Splenda®
¼ cup egg substitute or 1 large
   egg

2 large egg whites, lightly beaten
1 teaspoon lemon zest
⅔ cup non fat sweetened
   condensed milk
1 ½ cups plain organic non fat
   yogurt
¼ teaspoon salt
2 teaspoons vanilla extract
1 tablespoon powdered sugar,
   for dusting

Preheat oven to 300°. Lightly oil an 8-inch square cake pan or coat it with nonstick cooking spray.

In a mixing bowl, stir together flour, Splenda®, cinnamon, baking powder and salt with a fork. Add oil, egg whites, margarine, and half of the vanilla. Mix with a fork until well blended. Press into the bottom of the prepared pan.

In a mixing bowl, whisk together egg substitute, condensed milk and cornstarch until smooth. Add the yogurt and whisk until smooth. Blend in lemon zest ad the remaining vanilla. Pour over the crust. Evenly sprinkle blueberries over the top. Bake for 1 ¼ to 1 ½ hours, or until the top is just set. Let cool in the pan on a rack. Serve warm or chilled, dusted with powdered sugar.

There are many excellent putter fitting systems available to you at your local golf shop or club. A good fitting system will analyze your putter's shaft length and feel, the grip size and type, head design, loft, weight and visual aspects based on your individuality. Putting has been termed the most important part of the game by some, so take the time to select this crucial club for your best game.

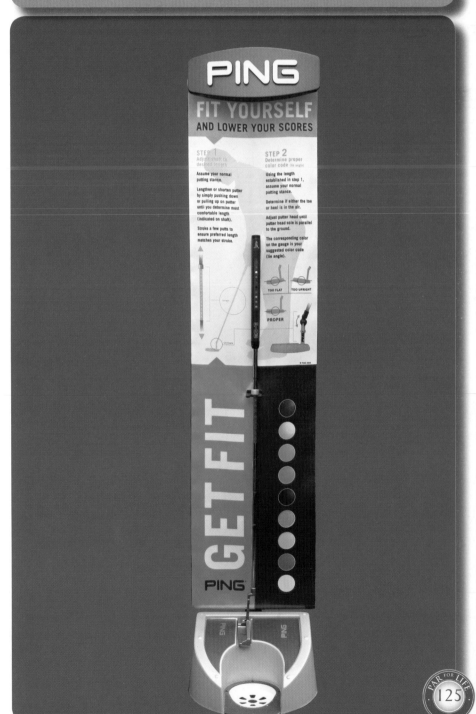

Player #6
Geneva National Golf Club, Lake Geneva, Wisconsin

The Exercise Recipes

In the Sides, Extras & Short Game chapter, we gave you Exercise Recipes for your specific body type. The following pages further explain each exercise, how to do it, when to do it and how long to do it.

No matter which category of golfer you are - Out of Bounds, In the Rough or Need Greens in Regulation, there are some instructions to keep in mind throughout every exercise.

1 - When standing, always make sure your feet are hip width apart and pointing mostly straight forward. Your feet, knees, hips and shoulders should be in alignment.

2 - We always want you to balance your weight evenly on both sides of your body, no matter if you are standing, sitting or lying down. Check that your weight is even both front to back and right to left.

3 - We want both sides of your body working at the same pace. You may find while performing an exercise that your right arm and shoulder, for example, moves more fluidly or quickly than your left. Get both sides moving at the same pace. This is what we call bilateral function, a necessary property for any golfer.

4 - Keep movements slow. In many exercises we are trying to get all of the smaller, supporting muscles doing their job, and we do not want the big muscles or gravity taking over.

These exercises are designed to get your body into a more proper alignment and increase your function. We are not going for speed, nor are we directly impacting your cardio-vascular health or strength. In these recipes we are whispering to the body, and it will hear the message!

As you work with the Par For Life Institute, we will continue to challenge you, adding exercise recipes as well as strength training that are designed to keep your body functional and strong throughout your life. For the Front Nine, however, we need to master the basics, and a body that is truly bilaterally functional will last for years.

Trevino #6
Geneva National Golf Club
Lake Geneva, Wisconsin

In the Rough Exercise Recipe

If your self-assessment has brought you to the conclusion that you have an anterior pelvic tilt, then you are an "IN THE ROUGH" golfer. Most likely, your illiopsoas muscle, the main muscle that connects your upper body to your lower body, is overly tight, causing your lumbar spine to become closer to the front of your femur, thus pulling your pelvis forward. This deviation from the body's design ultimately leads to other compensating deviations. This Recipe is designed to get your pelvis back into a more neutral position.

1 - Back Settle. *Relax for 5 Minutes*

2 - Standing Shoulder Shrugs - *30 repetitions*

3 - Back Settle Reverse Presses - *30 repetitions*

4 - Standing Shoulder Rolls -

    30 repitions each, forward and back

5 - Standing Arm Circles -

    40 repitions each, forward and back

6 - Back Settle Pullovers - *30 repetitions*

7 - Lay Back Gluteal Contractions - *60 repetitions*

8 - Lay Back Knee Pillow Squeezes - *60 repetitions*

9 - Foot Circles, Point & Flexes -

    40 repetitions each direction

10 - Supine Groin Stretch - *15 minutes per side*

11 - Wall Sit - *2 minutes*

This should take you about 45 minutes, and is best done in the morning. If that's too much time, do exercises 1-9 and 11 in the morning, and save the Supine Groin Stretch for the evening.

The Back Settle is a must-have exercise for anyone who has ever felt a twinge in their back, and its a passive exercise, so no exertion is necessary.

Find a chair, couch or block that you can lay next to. Lay on your back with your behind and the back of your upper legs resting against the side of the block, and your lower leg in a 90° angle on the top of the block. Ideally, both your hips and knees are bent at a 90° angle.

Make sure your feet are pointing to the ceiling, your head is resting on the ground, relaxed, and your arms are relaxed out to your side with your palms facing the ceiling. Relax your abdominals and upper body as you allow your hips to simply relax.

In the Rough 2 –
Standing Shoulder Shrugs

Stand with your feet hip width apart, your toes pointed straight forward, your knees locked and your quadriceps tight. With your arms at your sides, lift your shoulders up to your ears and back down. Repeat this 40 times, keeping your lower body from swaying forward or back.

One key to this exercise is to try to relax your head and neck through the motions. Keep your shoulders back, not necessarily pinching your shoulder blades together, but back so that you do not have a slouched appearance. As you bring your shoulders up, concentrate on making the motion with your shoulders only to avoid the tendency of tightening your neck.

In the Rough 3 –
Back Settle Reverse Presses

Lie on your back with your legs on a chair in the Back Settle position. If a chair or ottoman is not handy, you can place your feet on a wall, but make sure your knees and hips are bent at a 90° angle and that your feet and knees remain hip width apart.

Place your elbows on the ground to the sides of your body with your fists up in the air.

From this position, squeeze your shoulder blades together, then release, 40 times. The motion may feel as if you are pushing your elbows into the ground, which is not the intended motion, but a normal sensation. With each squeeze and release, try to get a full range of motion through your shoulder blades and opening your chest.

In the Rough 4 - Standing Shoulder Rolls

Stand with your knees and feet directly under your hips and make sure your feet are pointed forward. Tighten your quadriceps, and take care to keep your lower body perfectly still throughout the exercise. With big motions, roll your shoulders in forward circles for forty repetitions. Reverse the motion and roll the shoulders backward for forty repetitions. Throughout the exercise, work to get a full range of motion in the shoulders and the scapular area.

In the Rough 5 - Standing Arm Circles

Stand with your feet directly under your hips and your quadriceps held tight. Bend your fingertips to your palms and lock your thumb straight. Pinch your shoulder blades together and lift your arms up to shoulder height, parallel with the floor and palms down. Holding your quads tight and keeping your lower body stable, circle your arms forward for forty repetitions. Roll your arms back with your thumbs pointed backward and your palms up, and circle backward forty times. This exercise serves to open up your chest, shoulders and thoracic spine, putting them into a more functional position.

In the Rough 6 - Back Settle Pullovers

Lie on your back with your legs on a chair or an ottoman in the Back Settle position. Clasp your hands together over your head, and keep your elbows locked throughout the exercise.
Slowly bring both arms to the floor, then lift them back up toward your knees, stopping short of your knees. Repeat this 40 times.
You should concentrate on keeping the movement slow throughout every repetition. This will help to train all of the small supporting muscles in the shoulder and chest to do the work rather than the large muscles and gravity taking over as they often do.

In the Rough 7 -
Lay Back Gluteal Contractions

Lie on your back with your knees bent, and make sure that your feet are pointed straight forward with your knees and feet hip-width apart. In this exercise, you will be contracting and releasing your Gluteal muscles sixty times. It sounds simple, but isolating the glutes may prove to be more challenging than you would think. Make sure your abdominal muscles remain relaxed and don't work to assist. Your pelvis should not move during these contractions. Have someone watch you - they should not see any movement except maybe your upper hamstring right where it attaches to your behind.

Once you isolate you gluteal muscles, then you can work on making sure both the right and left sides fire at the same time with the same intensity.

In the Rough 8 -
Lay Back Knee Pillow Squeezes

Lie on your back with your knees bent, and make sure that your feet are pointed straight forward with your knees and feet hip-width apart. Place a pillow or a rolled towel between your knees, and squeeze and release the pillow sixty times.

Make sure both your left and right knees are squeezing at the same time and with the same intensity.

Throughout the exercise, relax your abdominals, back and shoulders. Your pelvis should not move during the squeezes.

Lie on your back with both legs extended. Make sure your knees and feet are hip width apart, and your toes are pointed straight up. Tighten up your left quadricep, and pick up your right leg comfortably behind your knee. Relax your abdominals, back and shoulders as you circle your right foot forty times to the right. Then circle the same foot forty times to the left, then point your toe and flex your foot back forty times. Straighten and tighten your right leg, lift your left leg, and perform the circles and point-flexes on the left side.

In the Rough 10 -
Supine Groin Stretch

Lie on your back with only one leg up on the chair or ottoman. This leg should be bent in a 90° angle at both the hip and knee. Your other leg should be straight out on the floor. Throughout the stretch, keep both legs straight out from the hip joint with your toes pointed upwards. Relax your arms out at about a 45° angle from your shoulders with your palms up. This allows your shoulders to fully relax into the ground. Relax in this position for at least 5 minutes on each side, and up to 15 minutes per side for the greatest benefits.

In the Rough 11 -
Wall Sit

The Wall Sit is a demanding exercise, but is also an easy position to achieve if you are not able to lay down. If your lower back aches on the golf course, you can even do a quick Wall Sit against your golf cart mid-round. Place your back against a wall and slide down until you have a 90° angle at your hips and knees, as if you are sitting on a chair. Flatten your low back into the wall and hold this position for one minute or more.

Out of Bounds 1 - Back Settle

The Back Settle is a must-have exercise for anyone who has ever felt a twinge in their back, and its a passive exercise, so no exertion is necessary.

Find a chair, couch or block that you can lay next to. Lay on your back with your behind and the back of your upper legs resting against the side of the block, and your lower leg in a 90° angle on the top of the block. Ideally, both your hips and knees are bent at a 90° angle.

Make sure your feet are pointing to the ceiling, your head is resting on the ground, relaxed, and your arms are relaxed out to your side with your palms facing the ceiling. Relax your abdominals and upper body as you allow your hips to simply relax.

Out of Bounds Exercise Menu

If your self evaluation has shown that you have elevations and rotations in your joints, but your pelvis is in a fairly neutral position, you are in our second category of golfers. This exercise recipe is designed to reduce the disparities in your posture, and get your right and left sides working together to restore the bilateral function of our body design.

1 - Back Settle - *Relax for 5 minutes*
2 - Standing Windmill - *10 repetitions of 4 positions*
3 - Gravity Drop - *Hold for 3 minutes*
4 - Pelvic Tilts - *10 repetitions foward and back*
5 - Lay Back Gluteal Contractions - *60 repetitions*
6 - Lay Back Knee Pillow Squeezes - *60 repetitions*
7 - Foot Circles & Point-Flexes -
      40 repetitions each side
8 - X-Factor Twist - *Hold for 2 minutes each side*
9 - Wall Sit - *Hold for 2 minutes*

This recipe should take about 20 minutes.

If you have determined that in addition to rotations and/or elevations in your joints, you also show that your hips have an anterior tilt (In the Rough), or a posterior tilt (Needs Greens in Regulations), you may consider adding a Supine Groin Stretch to this recipe. Perform the stretch after the X-Factor Twist and before the Wall Sit. If you have a posterior pelvic tilt, consider adding a rolled up towel under your lumbar spine during the stretch.

Stand with your feet and knees hip width apart and tighten your quadriceps. Extend both arms out to the side and lock your elbows and wrists. Moving only from your waist, and keeping your entire body in a straight plane (as if your body is completely against a wall), bend to your right and then your left five times per side. You may be fighting your body to stay on plane.

After the first set, widen your stance about six inches and repeat the exercise.

After the second set, make your feet wider still, keeping your toes pointed forward, and repeat the exercise.

For the last set, get your feet right under your hips just like the first set and repeat the exercise.

Out of Bounds 3 - Gravity Drop

Stand on a stair or the back of your golf cart with your toes on the stair and your heels off of the stair. Make sure that you keep your body in alignment - shoulders over hips over knees over ankles, and drop your weight through your heels so that you are balancing on the balls of your feet and your heels are lower than your toes. The immediate stretch is felt in your calves, but as you hold this stretch for a minute and make sure that you are not leaning forward or back, the benefits your body will reap is much greater. As you settle in this stretch, your joints can come back into alignment and your hips settle in a very functional position.

If you like the way this stretch feels, you may want to invest in a Slant Board. A slant board allows you to do the gravity drop against a wall while standing on the board, letting your hips and joints settle into a very functional position.

Out of Bounds 4 - Pelvic Tilts

Lie on your back with your feet and knees hip-width apart and your knees bent. Make sure your feet are pointed straight forward. Relax your upper body into the floor. Moving only your pelvis, roll your hips forward so that you create a big arch in your back, then roll it backward, flattening your back into the floor.

When we golf, we torque our spines to one side and then another. Since our sport demands that we continue this twisting spinal motion, Pelvic Tilts are a great exercise that gets our spine, the lumbar spine in particular, moving front to back again. On the golf course, pelvic tilts may not always be pratical, but standing or sitting Cats & Dogs are a great way to keep your back moving and functional throughout your round.

Lie on your back with your knees bent, and make sure that your feet are pointed straight forward with your knees and feet hip-width apart. In this exercise, you will be contracting and releasing your Gluteal muscles sixty times. It sounds simple, but isolating the glutes may prove to be more challenging than you would think. Make sure your abdominal muscles remain relaxed and don't work to assist. Your pelvis should not move during these contractions. Have someone watch you - they should not see any movement except maybe your upper hamstring right where it attaches to your behind.

Once you isolate you gluteal muscles, then you can work on making sure both the right and left sides fire at the same time with the same intensity.

Lie on your back with your knees bent, and make sure that your feet are pointed straight forward with your knees and feet hip-width apart. Place a pillow or a rolled towel between your knees, and squeeze and release the pillow sixty times.

Make sure both your left and right knees are squeezing at the same time and with the same intensity.

Throughout the exercise, relax your abdominals, back and shoulders. Your pelvis should not move during the squeezes.

Out of Bounds 7 -
Foot Circles & Point-Flex

Lie on your back with both legs extended. Make sure your knees and feet are hip width apart, and your toes are pointed straight up. Tighten up your left quadricep, and pick up your right leg comfortably behind your knee. Relax your abdominals, back and shoulders as you circle your right foot forty times to the right. Circle the same foot forty times to the left, then point your toe and flex your foot back forty times.
Straighten and tighten your right leg, lift your left leg, and perform the circles and point-flexes on the left side.

Out of Bounds 8 -
The X-Factor Twist

Lie on your right side with your legs bent in a 90° angle at the hips and knees. Your arms are together and straight out from your shoulders. Firmly keep your knees and feet together in this position as you bring your left arm flat to the ground on your left side. Hold this for one minute, then repeat on your left side. You may find that one arm hits the floor, and the other doesn't even come close.

Out of Bounds 9 -
Wall Sit

Place your back against a wall and slide down until you have a 90° angle at your hips and knees, as if you are sitting on a chair. Flatten your low back into the wall and hold this position for one minute or more. The Wall Sit is a demanding exercise, but is also an easy position to achieve if you are not able to lay down. If your lower back aches on the golf course, you can even do a quick Wall Sit against your golf cart mid-round.

Need Greens in Regulation
Exercise Menu

If your self assessment has revealed that your pelvis shows a posterior pelvic tilt, you are in our third category of golfers. Traditionally a posterior tilt would indicate weakness - a sign of aging and "natural" body decay. We no longer take this view. True, aging and weakness will allow the pelvis to tilt under and the spine to curve forward. We find, however, that many strong athletes, including bicyclists, runners and pilates experts, put their low back and pelvis in a flexed position so often, that they develop a posterior tilt out of strength.

The following recipe is designed to return the posterior pelvis to a more neutral position:

1 - Standing Shoulder Rolls -
   30 repetitions forward and back

2 - Standing Arm Circles -
   40 repetitions forward and back

3 - Static Extension Position - *Hold for 1 minute*

4 - Lay Back Gluteal Contractions - *60 repetitions*

5 - Back Settle Reverse Presses - *30 repetitions*

6 - Lay Back Knee Pillow Squeezes - *60 repetitions*

7 - Lay Back Isolated Hip Flexor Lifts -
   60 repetitions each side

8 - Supine Gluteal Contractions - *60 repetitions*

9 - Foot Circles & Point-Flexes -
   40 repetitions each side

10 - Supine Groin with Towels - *Relax for 15 Minutes*

11 - Wall Sit- *Hold for 2 minutes*

This recipe should take you about 45 minutes, and is best done first thing in the morning to set yourself up for the day. If that's too long, skip#10 and do the Supine Groin Stretch later in the day.

Stand with your knees and feet directly under your hips and make sure your feet are pointed forward. Tighten your quadriceps, and take care to keep your lower body perfectly still throughout the exercise. With big motions, roll your shoulders in forward circles for forty repetitions. Reverse the motion and roll the shoulders backward for forty repetitions. Throughout the exercise, work to get a full range of motion in the shoulders and the scapular area.

Need Green in Regulation 2 - Standing Arm Circles

Stand with your feet directly under your hips and your quadriceps held tight. Bend your fingertips to your palms and lock your thumb straight. Pinch your shoulder blades together and lift your arms up to shoulder height, parallel with the floor and palms down. Holding your quads tight and keeping your lower body stable, circle your arms forward for forty repetitions. Roll your arms back with your thumbs pointed backward and your palms up, and circle backward forty times. This exercise serves to open up your chest, shoulders and thoracic spine, putting them into a more functional position.

Need Greens in Regulation 3 - Static Extension Position

Get on your hands and knees with your knees directly under your hips and your hands directly under your shoulders. Walk your hands forward about 8 inches, and shift your weight forward so that your shoulders are directly over your hands and your hips are forward of your knees. Hold this position with your elbows locked straight, bow your head slightly down and collapse your shoulders and your low back. Hold this position for one minute.

Need Greens in Regulation 4 - Lay Back Gluteal Contractions

Lie on your back with your knees bent, and make sure that your feet are pointed straight forward with your knees and feet hip-width apart. In this exercise, you will be contracting and releasing your Gluteal muscles sixty times. It sounds simple, but isolating the glutes may prove to be more challenging than you would think. Make sure your abdominal muscles remain relaxed and don't work to assist. Your pelvis should not move during these contractions. Have someone watch you - they should not see any movement except maybe your upper hamstring right where it attaches to your behind.

Need Greens in Regulation 5 - Back Settle Reverse Presses

Lie on your back with your legs on a chair in the Back Settle position. If a chair or ottoman is not handy, you can place your feet on a wall, but make sure your knees and hips are bent at a 90° angle and that your feet and knees remain hip width apart.

Place your elbows on the ground to the sides of your body with your fists up in the air.

From this position, squeeze your shoulder blades together, then release, 40 times. The motion may feel as if you are pushing your elbows into the ground, which is not the intended motion, but a normal sensation. With each squeeze and release, try to get a full range of motion through your shoulder blades and opening your chest.

Need Greens in Regulations 6 - Lay Back Knee Pillow Squeezes

Lie on your back with your knees bent, and make sure that your feet are pointed straight forward with your knees and feet hip-width apart. Place a pillow or a rolled towel between your knees, and squeeze and release the pillow sixty times.

Make sure both your left and right knees are squeezing at the same time and with the same intensity.

Throughout the exercise, relax your abdominals, back and shoulders. Your pelvis should not move during the squeezes.

Need Greens in Regulation 7 - Isolated Hip Flexor Lift

Lie on your back with your knees bent, and be sure to keep your feet and knees hip-width apart. Let your head, shoulders, back and abdominals relax as you begin to work your hip flexors without enlisting other muscles to help.

Rest your right leg up on your toe and hold your leg here to stabilize your hip. Lift your left leg up to a 90° degree angle to the floor then bring it back down to the floor. Repeat this exercise 40 times, making sure that the angle of your knee never changes, and that you lift no further than 90 degrees.

Need Greens in Regulation 8 - Supine Gluteal Contractions (not pictured)

Lie on your back with your legs extended. In this exercise, you will be contracting and releasing your Gluteal muscles sixty times. Take care through the entire exercise that your toes point upward. Make sure your abdominal muscles remain relaxed and don't work to assist. Your pelvis should not move during these contractions. Have someone watch you - they should not see any movement except maybe your upper hamstring right where it attaches to your behind.
You may find that this position is easier than if your knees were bent - or maybe more difficult. Once you isolate you gluteal muscles, then you can work on making sure both the right and left sides fire at the same time with the same intensity.

Need Greens in Regulation 9 - Foot Circles & Point-Flex

Lie on your back with both legs extended. Make sure your knees and feet are hip width apart, and your toes are pointed straight up. Tighten up your left quadricep, and pick up your right leg comfortably behind your knee. Relax your abdominals, back and shoulders as you circle your right foot forty times to the right. Then circle the same foot forty times to the left, then point your toe and flex your foot back forty times. Straighten and tighten your right leg, lift your left leg, and perform the circles and point-flexes on the left side.

Need Greens in Regulations 10 - Supine Groin on Towels

Lie on your back with only one leg up on a chair or automan. This leg should be bent at 90° angles both at the hip and knee. Your other leg should be straight out on the floor. Place a rolled towel underneath the small of your back so that your arch does not touch the ground. You want to feel the towel, but don't have the roll so large that it creates and uncomfortable arch. Throughout the stretch, keep both legs straight out from the hip joint with your toes pointed upwards. Relax your arms out at about a 45 degree angle from your shoulders with your palms up. This allows your shoulders to fully relax into the ground. Relax in this position for at least 5 minutes on each side, and up to 15 minutes per side for the greatest benefits.

Need Greens in Regulation 11 - Wall Sit

Place your back against a wall and slide down until you have a 90° angle at your hips and knees, as if you are sitting on a chair. Flatten your low back into the wall and hold this position for one minute or more. The Wall Sit is a demanding exercise, but is also an easy position to achieve if you are not able to lay down. If your lower back aches on the golf course, you can even do a quick Wall Sit against your golf cart mid-round.